Ideas at the Intersection of Mathematics, Philosophy, and Theology

Ideas at the Intersection of Mathematics, Philosophy, and Theology

Carlos R. Bovell

WIPF & STOCK · Eugene, Oregon

IDEAS AT THE INTERSECTION OF MATHEMATICS, PHILOSOPHY, AND THEOLOGY

Copyright © 2012 Carlos R. Bovell. All rights reserved. Except for brief quotations in critical publications or reviews, no part of this book may be reproduced in any manner without prior written permission from the publisher. Write: Permissions, Wipf and Stock Publishers, 199 W. 8th Ave., Suite 3, Eugene, OR 97401.

Wipf & Stock
An Imprint of Wipf and Stock Publishers
199 W. 8th Ave., Suite 3
Eugene, OR 97401
www.wipfandstock.com

ISBN 13: 978-1-4982-5862-3
Manufactured in the U.S.A.

*In loving memory of my father
who always supported me in my scholarly pursuits*

Contents

Preface ix

1 The definition of mathematics seems to limit its potential for the humanities / 1

2 Ninety-nine percent of mathematics has little to no use for philosophy / 11

3 Some ideas on Husserl's remarks that mathematicians are not pure theoreticians / 20

4 Some ideas on Heidegger and the influence of mathematics and science on metaphysics / 34

5 A comparison between Euclid and Aquinas and a question of method / 46

6 On the "good and necessary consequence" clause in the Westminster Confession of Faith (1647) / 57

7 Thoughts on supernaturalism and its irrelevance for science and mathematics / 66

8 Thoughts on the intermediate value theorem and the "knowledge-boundary" problem / 74

9 On the associative property of addition and its application to the Godhead / 82

10 Remarks on the search for an infinite God in the philosophy of Edmund Husserl / 99

11 Observations regarding the Kalam argument and its disavowal of actual infinites / 110

Bibliography / 123

Preface

WHEN I CHANGED MY major to math in college, I began to experience a radical disconnect between the kinds of things we would talk about in my math classes and the kinds of things we would talk about everywhere else. I remember wondering whether math and the rest of life might be a good example of what the late Stephen Jay Gould called, "non-overlapping magisteria." The situation was even more pronounced when I compared what we were talking about in my math courses with what we were talking about at the independent, "fundamental," Baptist church I was attending at the time. For a restless mind like mine, the lack of integration was bewildering. There just *had* to be fruitful ways for either bringing Christian faith to bear upon the math I was learning in college or for bringing the math I was learning in class to bear somehow on my faith.

My first attempts to look into this were met with a number of difficulties. For starters, I knew next to nothing about how to do academic research. Moreover, as a commuter student I had limited access to academic libraries and very little guidance for sifting through the scholarly literature. (Keep in mind this was *before* the internet took off and *before* electronic document delivery.) It took a couple of years to land some success in tracking down relevant sources. My initial impression was that—and this came as a surprise—there were relatively few people interested in finding places where Christian faith might intersect with mathematics. Moreover, the sources I had on hand were just not helpful for the kind of investigation I was intent on doing.

Some authors were convinced that the entire field of mathematics inherently depended on the truth of Christian religion for its disciplinary successes. If it were not for the validity of Christian theology, they argued, mathematics would never have been able to achieve any of its historical accomplishments. Other writers seemed too eager to conclude that because the Bible is the Word of God, it had to contain basic logical and mathematical truths from which logico-mathematical systems could

Preface

consistently be built. Still others sought to persuade readers that Christian scripture is not irrelevant to mathematics. In support of this claim, one writer culled "illustrations" of basic logic and mathematics from the stories of the Bible. Although the authors I read were more educated than I in both mathematics and theology, I could not shake the feeling that their treatments somehow left a lot to be desired. When it comes to the integration of mathematics and Christian faith, there is still plenty of work for us to do!

It is with the hope of spurring others on in their work that I agreed to publish the present book. Over the past decade or so, I have given a number of papers at academic conferences, most of which were exploratory in nature, seeking to draw mathematics, philosophy and theology into conversation. Although a handful of the essays have found their way into print, most remained on a flash key or computer drive somewhere, waiting to be rewritten, rethought, or simply deleted.

In the meantime, some professors who teach mathematics in Christian settings requested that I compile a collection of my talks for the benefit of their students who were writing senior theses. The professors expressed concern that there are too few resources available for math majors interested in writing senior papers on topics that integrate mathematics and Christian faith. This is something I certainly appreciate. So in spite of the fact that the papers are largely "unfinished," I have been encouraged to share them with students in order to give them some ideas for the integration of mathematics, philosophy and theology.

Thanks to the Wipf and Stock staff for accepting this project and agreeing to see it to print. Thanks also to the Reverend Harald Peeders who is always encouraging me in my work.

I express my sincerest appreciation to Jen—without her love, none of this would have been possible—and to Jamie, Elena, Mateo and Luisa, who are convinced that their father makes the best plátanos on the planet.

1

The definition of mathematics seems to limit its potential for the humanities

ANCIENT PHILOSOPHERS TENDED TO think that one should ask what a thing is before pondering whether it exists or how its existence bears upon this or that consideration. Perhaps contemporary interdisciplinary efforts, too, can benefit from asking what mathematics is before troubling with how its existence might impinge upon the humanities. Unfortunately, mathematicians themselves have no interest whatsoever in this question, settling instead for the *sociological* conclusion that mathematics is what mathematicians do. In this short essay, I explore some of the problems that beset this conclusion. I suggest that a reluctance to take the question, "What is x?," seriously diminishes the degree to which mathematics can inform and contribute to discussions in the humanities (and vice versa).

According to Socrates, the "What-is-x?" question is of central importance for doing legitimate philosophy. As such, it only admits of a very specific kind of answer. Even so, rarely does Socrates appear satisfied with the answers his interlocutors provide, try as they may to respond to his incessant questioning. Yet Socrates' chief virtue, in the eyes of many, is that he persists in asking the most interesting types of questions. Consider, for example, the following exchange (*Euthyphr.* 5d-6d):

> Socr. Tell me then, what do you say holiness is, and what unholiness?
> Euthr. Well then, I say that holiness is doing what I am doing now, prosecuting the wrongdoer . . .
> Socr. At present try to tell me clearly what I asked you just now. For my friend, you did not give me sufficient information before, when I asked what holiness was, but you told me that this was holy which you are now doing, prosecuting your father for murder.

Ideas at the Intersection of Mathmatics, Philosophy, and Theology

> Euthr. Well, what I said was true, Socrates.
>
> Socr. Perhaps. But, Euthyphro, you say that many other things are holy, do you not?
>
> Euthr. Why, so there are.
>
> Socr. Now call to mind that this is not what I asked you, to tell me one or two of the many holy acts, but to tell the essential aspect, by which all holy acts are holy; for you said that all unholy acts were unholy and all holy ones holy by one aspect. Or don't you remember?
>
> Euthr. I remember.
>
> Socr. Tell me then what this aspect is, that I may keep my eye fixed upon it and employ it as a model and, if anything you or anyone else does agrees with it, may say that the act is holy, and if not, that it is unholy.

In the end, Euthyphro becomes so bemused by Socrates' persistent questioning that he feels as if Daedalus is affecting his ability to answer, for whatever his reply, once it has been set down, it turns over into a new question.

Mathematicians, especially over the course of the last century, have come to feel something like Euthyphro in this regard. After attempting to provide satisfactory answers to the question, "What is mathematics?" they have had to watch their philosophical descriptions also turn into new questions. "The fact that the debate never really got resolved," explains Fernando Gouvêa, "together with the complicating factor of Gödel's incompleteness theorems, seem to have caused most mathematicians to lose interest."[1] When coordinating a recent anthology of commissioned essays in philosophy of mathematics, Bonnie Gold and Roger Simons were interested to know what researchers in mathematics education might contribute to a "What is mathematics?" section. Unfortunately, many of them were too busy to participate or declined their invitation to remark.[2] Nevertheless, the decision on the part of Gold and Simons to move in a mathematics *education* direction illustrates a wider cultural judgment: philosophy can no longer offer solutions to its most pressing traditional questions.

Such a negative observation tends to elicit two lines of response: 1) search elsewhere for answers to these questions, or 2) stop asking the

1. Gouvêa, "Review."
2. Gold and Simons, *Proof*, 265.

The definition of mathematics seems to limit its potential for the humanities

questions in the first place. Opting for the former, many scholars have begun looking to sociology, psychoanalysis, anthropology and cognitive science in order to gain new insight. Others have taken up economics, politics, cultural criticism, and researches in organization, policy, and pedagogy. Alternatively, not a few practitioners are turning a blind eye toward the traditional issues, issues that have grounded and guided intellectual inquiry over the course of its history in the West. Simply put, these questions are now being ignored by the wider academic community because such questions come across as ultimately unanswerable, or, if not that, then philosophically meaningless.

To illustrate the point, Mura reports that a full one-third of professors she surveyed did not offer answers to the question, "What is mathematics?"[3] This finding is indicative of broader cultural trends. Such negative responses have had a profound impact upon the philosophy of mathematics, programmatically impacting the types of questions philosophers of mathematics view as fruitful to ask. All of these trends will have direct implications for what mathematics might try to say to the humanities.

From a philosophical point of view, Moser has taken a hard look at the Greek "what is x?" question and concluded that philosophers should consider redirecting their focus if they want philosophy to thrive in contemporary culture. Philosophy should change, Moser suggests, from focusing on providing "agnostic-resistant reasons to a kind of support that is avowedly perspectival, relative to a theorist's (variable) semantic commitments and relevant purposes in theorizing."[4] His view is that philosophical inquiry no longer needs to occupy itself with trying to answer agnostic objections.[5] In other words, recent developments in epistemology and philosophy of language give philosophers warrant for providing explanations perspectivally, explanations that can only be judged as relevant with respect to a theorist's semantic commitments, explanatory ends, and practical means for achieving those ends.

Accordingly, mathematicians' philosophical respite from the "what is mathematics?" question is not only culturally perceptive, but also theoretically justified. In other words, it may be enough for mathematicians

---

3. Mura, "Images," 382.
4. Moser, *Philosophy*, 58.
5. Moser, *Philosophy*, 58–59.

to simply come up with explanations that are meaningful to working mathematicians. For example, R. S. D. Thomas, in his essay "Mathematics as the Science of Relations as Such," clarifies that he is not concerned with solving philosophical problems. On the contrary, he hopes to *have* philosophical problems, but ones that actually address issues that pertain to activities he can recognize as mathematical.[6] This suggests that if one is interested in knowing what mathematics is, then one should begin by looking at the types of activities in which mathematicians regularly engage. And if one has no interest in such things then, all the better, for as Hersh quips, "You don't need to know what is meant by 'one' in order to know that one and one is two."[7] Hellman explains: "The point is that working mathematicians typically have not reflected on exactly what their commitments are, or, if they have, they have come to many different individual conclusions, some very far from a 'face-value reading.'"[8] Moser reports something similar regarding what philosophers think about philosophy.[9]

In my view, this poses a bit of a quandary for any who would like to see mathematics dialogue with the humanities, a quandary that seems to stem, at least in part, from what Moser calls "self-referential worries." For example, consider the following observation made by Grozdev, Derzhanski, and Sendova: "At times one hears that mathematics is what mathematicians do, and a mathematician is someone who doesn't ask what mathematics is about . . . Somewhat of a vicious circle isn't it?"[10] Similarly, Thurston writes, ". . . what mathematicians are accomplishing is to advance human understanding of mathematics. . . . It may sound almost circular to say that . . ."[11] Yet Thurston ventures to inquire further and ponders whether the fundamental circularity that obtains from this approach to our question arises precisely because mathematics is an essentially recursive discipline.

6. Thomas, "Extreme Science," 255.
7. Hersh, "Review."
8. Hendricks and Leitgeb, *Philosophy*, 152.
9. He writes, "At a level of specificity, notions of inquiry and of philosophy are perhaps as many as the theorists wielding a notion of inquiry or philosophy. It would be rash, in any case, to propose any single thing called 'the' notion of inquiry or of philosophy." See Moser, *Philosophy*, 226.
10. Grozdev, Derzhanski, and Sendova, "For Those."
11. Thurston, "On Proof," 162.

The definition of mathematics seems to limit its potential for the humanities

One way to analyze this is to appreciate that doing mathematics is a first-order activity whereas inquiring into what mathematics is is a second-order activity. Discussions treating the relationship between first- and second-order activities go at least as far back as Plato. Yet perhaps there is something that can prove instructive here concerning Socrates' dissatisfaction with first-order answers to second-order questions. Socrates seems correct to surmise that his second-order questions are of a rather different sort than their first-order counterparts. In much the same way, any answer that boils down to "mathematics is what mathematicians do" will miss something that the "what is mathematics?" question is trying to get at. (Recall Euthyphro's answer above.) This is expressed in yet another way in the platonic dialogue, *Meno*. In it, the following observation is made: "Do you see what a captious argument you are introducing—that, forsooth, a man cannot inquire either about what he knows or about what he does not know? For he cannot inquire about what he knows, because he knows it…or again can he inquire about what he does not know, since he does not know about what he is to inquire." Compare this with an observation made by one mathematics education researcher: "Mathematics education researchers agreed a long time ago that mathematics comes to schools reincarnated (didactically transposed) as a 'subject matter' and they take it as a matter of fact that while '*mathematics* is mathematician's business, schools have *maths*' (Noss 1994)."[12] But which one, mathematics or maths, is the one that should interact with the humanities?

A survey of books on mathematics quickly shows that a mathematics/maths distinction can be difficult to uphold in practice. As one introductory book on mathematical reasoning claims: "Writing a proof is not separate from discovering the proof in the way that writing up a scientific experiment is separate from carrying out the experiment or performing a piece of music is separate from composing it. Attempts to write out a proof are an important part of the discovery process."[13] In many cases this proves true because, as Sieg makes clear: "Proofs provide explanations of what they prove by putting their conclusions in a context that shows them to be correct."[14] Yet we are reminded that there is something more going on than initially meets the eye when we encounter apologies given for

---

12. Sfard, "Many Faces," 506.
13. Eccles, *Introduction*, x.
14. Hendricks and Leitgeb, *Philosophy*, 243.

various choices that are made for specific presentations of mathematics in the interest of making proofs for theorems more elegant. For example, Spivak, in his text, *Calculus on Manifolds*, explains that "There are good reasons why the theorems should all be easy and the definitions hard. As the evolution of Stokes' Theorem revealed, a single simple principle can masquerade as several difficult results. . . . Concentrating the depth of a subject in the definitions is undeniably economical, but it is bound to produce some difficulties for the student. I hope the reader will be encouraged to learn Chapter 4 thoroughly by the assurance that the results will justify the effort."[15] Pascal once remarked that the success of geometry depended upon the way that definitions are emptied of all meaning, "having no other than that which one decides to give it."[16] And Montaigne before him complained that geometers have the ability to lead one wherever they wish to lead them by setting down definitions and axioms ahead of time that govern the ensuing discussion in whatever way they see fit.[17]

It would appear then that there are at least two vantage points to emphasize when one wishes to talk about mathematics. First, one can emphasize the *content* of a branch of mathematics that has already been thoroughly worked out. In this case, answers already laid down are given primacy and the questions that first elicited them occupy the background. Second, one can emphasize the *problems* of mathematics which have not yet been sorted through (or as if they had not yet been sorted through). In these cases, questions come to the fore and the answers fall by the wayside, for the answers' potential meanings are yet to be determined.[18] Martinez observes further that oftentimes at the forefront of mathematics very profound questions arise that defy immediate solution, but for various reasons they quickly become neglected and in many cases forgotten.[19] Gray remarks that at least since the Modern period these two perspectives on mathematics have gone "in and out of fashion."[20]

What prospect is there then for a meaningful exchange between mathematicians and the humanists? In light of the situation described

---

15. Spivak, *Calculus*, 3.
16. Pascal, *Pascal Selections*, 175.
17. de Montaigne, *Complete Works*, 403.
18. Compare Byers, *How Mathematicians*, 1–17.
19. Martinez, *Negative Math*, 7.
20. Gray, *Plato's Ghost*, 453.

The definition of mathematics seems to limit its potential for the humanities

above, the creation of an interdisciplinary domain where mathematics and the humanities can interchange might be fraught with some difficulty. For starters, a widespread tendency within mathematics to concentrate exclusively on what it is that mathematicians are already doing may cause a deliberately humanistic approach to mathematics to appear exceedingly unnatural or, at the very least, uncomfortably forced. Such negative opinions can range from seeing the endeavor as an obvious interdisciplinary contrivance to seeing the effort as an outright farce. Another difficulty may lie in the observation that the questions mathematicians are most interested in asking are mainly intramural ones such as how appropriate are the methods that are being employed? What is the most fruitful way to conceive a problem? And what kind of explanation should mathematicians regard as acceptable?[21] It is not immediately apparent how the humanities can directly illuminate such explicitly mathematical concerns. A further potential area of attention is the viability of an interdisciplinary, discursive space where mathematicians might collaborate with other non-scientific disciplines.

For example, the Dartmouth College summary of their "Mathematics across the Humanities" initiative included art, music, literature, history, and philosophy among the humanities. The summary report asserts: "The interdisciplinary rationale has several entailments. First, it requires looking at one's discipline in a fresh way, looking less for the most important concepts than for productive points of linkage, those that can form one end of a bridge to the other discipline."[22] According to the report, two of the main objectives for rethinking one's discipline in a deliberate, interdisciplinary fashion are to increase interest in mathematics within a more diverse student population and to provide non-math majors with other options than calculus and statistics for meeting their mathematics course requirements. One might note that these are wholly pragmatic motivations and then argue that as such they are for the most part external to mathematics proper. On principle, an objection might be lodged to the effect that in cases like this philosophy (or sometimes ideology) is being allowed to dictate to mathematics how it should be practiced. Shapiro calls this a "philosophy-first perspective" of mathematics. He argues a point that seems to apply here with greater or lesser force: "It is

21. Compare Gray, *Plato's Ghost*, 441.
22. Korey, "Dartmouth College," 25.

mathematics that is to be interpreted, and not what a prior (or a priori) philosophical theory says that mathematics should be."[23] To be fair, Shapiro acknowledges that his criticism can easily cut both ways. Still, it seems appropriate for the present discussion to mention this type of objection as a potential area of concern.

One last difficulty worth discussing suggests that it may prove unrealistic to expect adequate expertise in both mathematics and a humanistic discipline requisite for facilitating sustained interdisciplinary interaction. For example, a common complaint among mathematicians regarding the philosophy of mathematics is that the philosophers who engage in philosophy of mathematics are often not versed well enough in mathematics to make meaningful contributions. The same has been said about mathematicians doing philosophy. Another ongoing dispute surrounds whether history of mathematics should be done by historians or mathematicians. Mathematicians lament that historians do not know enough of the mathematics involved for an accurate historical account. Historians conversely regret that mathematicians do not evince a familiarity with proper historical method in their scholarship. Furthermore, when two cognitive scientists set out to describe mathematics through their discipline, a mathematician raised questions about the cognitive scientists' knowledge of mathematics. By way of response, the cognitive scientists addressed the mathematician's inadequate understanding of cognitive science.[24]

That said, many schools are actively seeking to humanize mathematics by presenting mathematical concepts in the context of real-life problems. According to the *Boston Globe* and other media sources, Harvard University is among several educational institutions that have bought into the idea that without real world contexts for the material being learned in mathematics classrooms, students will not be able to take home meaningful concepts from the class meetings. "Just as one doesn't become a marathon runner by reading about the Boston Marathon, so, too, one doesn't become a good problem solver by listening to lectures or reading about statistics," wrote the members of the task force. Professors teaching general education courses should, as much as possible, apply the academic concepts they teach "to the solution of concrete problems, the

---

23. Hendricks and Leitgeb, *Philosophy*, 224–226.
24. See Gold, "Review," and Lakoff and Nuñez, "Reader Review."

The definition of mathematics seems to limit its potential for the humanities

accomplishment of specific tasks, and the creation of actual objections and out-of-classroom experiences."[25]

This approach appears to hold some genuine promise. The Dartmouth initiative mentioned above would also fit in here. If mathematics is simply what mathematicians do, all that needs to happen to affect change is for mathematics to be done a little differently. Then, by definition, mathematicians' conception of mathematics will have to change. If students are consistently taught mathematics in such a way that it is presented to them as a fundamentally historical discipline, gradually developing in the context of real human problems, then it should only be a matter of time before what mathematicians did became more humanistic.

Even so, potential difficulties may arise. One would involve the amount of mathematics that may be required before being able to contrive concrete problems of practical application. If I may speak from my experience as a basic skills teacher, many of the real-world application problems that I have encountered in pre-algebra, algebra and pre-calculus textbooks are so obviously contrived that they have actually convinced some of my students that the mathematics they are learning is absolutely useless to them. One problem is that unless every set of exercises is specifically tailored to individual student interests, students will become convinced that only very limited domains of mathematics are actually applicable to them. If I might also speak from my experience as a student, it was disillusioning to learn that the interesting problems covered in my advanced differential equations course, for example, were not realistic because the mathematics required to tackle actual real-life scenarios demand a level of competence *beyond* that level achieved by the time of doctoral research. Only with the introduction of a substantial amount of additional mathematics would the real-world applications become somewhat feasible.

Another concern may stem from the conviction that mathematics is very different from every other discipline in the way that it offers certain proof for numerous mathematical assertions. To downplay such a central aspect of mathematics in favor of its more practical effects may contribute to a widespread ignorance of mathematical technique and reasoning. In addition, many mathematical concepts are not primarily rooted in real world experience. How then can real-world examples provide an

---

25. See, for example, Bombardieri, "Real-world Studies."

appropriate avenue for their introduction and exploration? This is not to say that these and similar concerns cannot satisfactorily be addressed, but they have been the grist for the mill in many faculty discussions and thus seem to merit further consideration. Lastly, an emphasis on practical applications may reinforce the cultural *ethos* that only what is immediately relevant is worthy of attention. This can result in a practical denial that mathematical inquiry has intrinsic validity.

To sum up, when mathematics is perceived principally in terms of what mathematicians do, it may prove difficult to facilitate a mathematics-humanities cooperative. For an interdisciplinary dialogue would expect mathematics to "[look] less for the most important concepts than for productive points of linkage" between mathematics and the humanities.[26] Yet if mathematics is understood largely in terms of the activities in which mathematicians presently engage *vis-à-vis* what mathematics *is* then, deprived of a distinctly mathematical self-understanding, it may prove difficult for mathematicians to participate meaningfully in interdisciplinary discussions. In other words, if mathematicians insist that there is no essence, whether metaphysical or practical, to the discipline their various activities are said to comprise, there will be little overarching direction for mathematics to offer to the interdisciplinary effort at hand.[27]

---

26. Korey, "Dartmouth College," 25.

27. This paper was presented at the conference, "Science, Technology and the Humanities," held at Stevens Institute of Technology, Hoboken, New Jersey, April, 2009.

2

Ninety-nine percent of mathematics has little to no use for philosophy

IN *HOW PROFESSORS THINK: The Curious World of Academic Judgment*, Michèle Lamont explains that she has come across four main opinions of philosophy current among academicians: "1) philosophers live in a world apart from other humanists, 2) nonphilosophers have problems evaluating philosophical work, and they are often perceived by philosophers as not qualified to do so, 3) philosophers do not explain the significance of their work, and 4) increasingly, what philosophers do is irrelevant, sterile, and self-indulgent."[1] While Lamont draws attention to the second opinion, my concern is with the fourth, what I call, "the fourth view." Why would an academic come to think that philosophy is irrelevant to what academics do? If philosophy proves to be sterile and self-indulgent, is this a poor reflection on philosophy or on some of the other disciplines?

On the face of it, this fourth view seems to hold philosophy in disdain, but the conclusion might express an important insight. Clearly, not all who hold this opinion have come to it uncritically. Some will base their view on their experience and exposure to philosophy, whether participating in interdisciplinary endeavors involving philosophers or reading works in philosophy. For example, a paper on set theory published in the *Notices of the American Mathematical Society* reminds readers—almost as a matter of course—that "[t]he philosophy of mathematics has little or no influence upon 99% of mathematics."[2] No noticeable disdain in this remark, only the observation that, as far as the author can see, philosophy's influence confines itself to the deciding of axioms in set theory.

---

1. Lamont, *How Professors Think*, 64.
2. Mycielski, "System of Axioms," 206.

Ideas at the Intersection of Mathmatics, Philosophy, and Theology

As one who studies and teaches philosophy, I find myself wanting and expecting philosophy to have more far-reaching effects on other academic disciplines. I wonder: why isn't philosophy's influence more greatly appreciated? Why would a non-philosopher see philosophy as inconsequential to what practitioners do in their respective fields? What is it about philosophy that causes non-philosophers to say that philosophers work "in their own stratosphere"?[3] How many disciplines are there that can honestly say, "99% of (insert discipline) is not influenced by philosophy"? Is there merit to this fourth view?

In the textbook I use in my intro classes, philosophy is defined from at least four perspectives. The author explains that some philosophers conceive of philosophy as the search for self-understanding. Others uphold the traditional view of philosophy as the love of wisdom. Furthermore, in the analytic tradition especially, philosophers consider it their business to subject our most basic concepts to rigorous, critical examination. Lastly, philosophy is regularly called upon to help adjudicate among competing positions with considerations of rational justification.[4] Compare these four aspects of philosophy with my students' own preconceived notions of philosophy: "Philosophy is a subject where you try to get to the truth of things." "Philosophy is a disciplined way of trying to keep an open mind." "Philosophy is the formulation of one's opinion on life." "Philosophy is about learning how to think deeply." "Philosophy is a way to understand the world better." "Philosophy is where one learns how to use logic and be more rational." As far as I am concerned, on the face of it there is not that great a difference between the textbook's definitions and the ones commonly offered by my students.[5]

If both non-philosophy professors and first year students have more or less the same understanding of what we are referring to when we talk about philosophy, then—all things being equal—one might expect both parties to have similar things to say about philosophy. However, when I ask my students, "When do you think a person would ever need to use philosophy?" they almost never reply, "Philosophy is not useful at all. In fact, it's irrelevant, sterile, and self-indulgent." Granted, I am their teacher and they are my students (the usual teacher-student social dynamics are in play), but this is not typically what they say. To the contrary, students

---

3. At least in the words of one historian. See Lamont, *How Professors Think*, 68.
4. Lawhead, *Philosophical Journey*, 4–8.
5. Here I see an example of philosophy and common sense coinciding.

invariably respond that philosophy is used *all the time*. Why? "Because if philosophy is about thinking, and every human being thinks, people are using philosophy every time they talk or think." Well said! This is reminiscent of the pragmatist C. I. Lewis: "It is—I take it—a distinguishing character of philosophy that it is everybody's business."[6] I whole-heartedly agree, but if it is everyone's business, why do non-philosophy academics think that philosophy is in its own stratosphere, being practiced in a world apart—even from the humanities? If, as Lewis explains, everyone can and must be their own philosopher, why is it that, after a semester of lively class discussions and working through representative philosophical texts, any number of students wind up agreeing with the fourth view of philosophy? What does this fourth view reveal about philosophy? In this chapter, I try to shed light on this question. Unfortunately, the answers I come up with point to more difficult questions still, which I take to be indicative of the problem at hand.

To begin, let us propose a distinction between *doing* and *reflecting*, one that will hold even when reflecting is what one is doing. Acknowledging that my efforts to define will include examples we cannot accept and leave out examples that are accepted, I offer the following descriptions. Doing might be described as a peculiar kind of first-person, first-order activity. An individual or group of individuals is doing when they are immediately (as opposed to mediately) engaged in domain-specified processes that comply with an indefinite range of pre-understood procedures for an indefinite range of pre-understood purposes. The experience associated with doing has an unmistakably, immediate quality to it that typifies it is as direct, first-order, and first-person. For example, if one "does" a sport (is actually participating), one is carrying out a certain range of domain-specified actions. Yet the particular aspect of doing that is germane here is that part of doing marked by a special, immediate kind of experience, a first-order type of engagement that has performance as its primary locus. The experience characteristic of doing is typically more subjectively, more existentially, and more physically *immediate* insofar as the participants' awareness is directly and almost completely devoted to the carrying out of appropriate actions or procedures.

By contrast, if doing can be described as a first-order activity, reflecting can be thought of as a second-order activity since its experiential quality is once-removed, so to speak, from the doing which it contemplates.

6. Lewis, *Mind and World Order*, 2.

Reflecting might still qualify as a first-person activity, at least in a way, since one can always say that there is an "I" that is doing the reflecting. However, pointing this out actually illustrates the first-order/second-order differential that I presently wish to draw out. In this case, the object of one's reflections is reconfigured as third-person doing. Reflecting begins the moment the "I," having done something and in a position to reflect, is subsumed into a third-person vantage which purports to be representative of any subject who is doing.

For example, there is a difference between doing mathematics and reflecting upon mathematics (mathematics, interestingly enough, being defined by mathematicians as "what mathematicians do").[7] When one does mathematics, one might seek answers to questions such as: What does the solution set to all differential equations of this or that form look like? Does such and such function have any critical points and if so, what are they? Is it true that any integer whose digits add up to three will be divisible by three? How can we write the decimal number 1, 234, 567 in a base 5 number system? Do all game theoretic scenarios have at least two Nash equilibriums? And so on. Contrast these questions with those asked by someone reflecting on mathematics: What is the ontological status of a solution set? If a function is said to be continuous and defined for all real numbers, do we traverse an actual infinite (the continuum) every time we evaluate it? What qualifies as a proof? Do proofs need to be checked before they are accepted? Would it be worthwhile for someone to find out under what circumstances two or more Nash equilibriums will exist, or are only the scenarios that have a single equilibrium the ones that matter? What axioms should we use for set theory and why?

The first series of questions exemplifies those that come up in the course of doing mathematics, while the latter are those that can come up while reflecting on mathematics. To many philosophers, philosophy has been greatly helped by realizing that most questions associated with reflecting could not be meaningfully asked until *after* some doing has already been done. As C. I. Lewis noted almost a century ago: "Action precedes reflection and even precision of behavior commonly outruns precision of thought—fortunately for us." Fortunately indeed! Yet C. I. Lewis would go so far as to say that for precisely this reason—that philosophy waits, as

---

7. Compare what I say here with Lange's remarks regarding the claim that philosophy is what philosophers do (or, at least, what they do in their capacity as philosophers). See Lange, *Cognitivity Paradox*.

it were, for the data to be brought in by some other kind of doing—philosophy should never be construed as having discovered something new. On the contrary, philosophy properly done will occupy itself with the examination of things already known, with the critical analysis of what is already familiar: "Just this business of bringing to clear consciousness and expressing coherently the principles which are implicitly intended in our dealing with the familiar is the distinctively philosophic enterprise."[8]

This raises an interesting question: What does philosophy contribute to the general store of knowledge? (Or better yet, *can* philosophy contribute anything to the general store of knowledge?) Dummett, for one, agrees that the critical examination of what is already known is what philosophy is principally about, yet he appears to want to leave some room for various kinds of philosophical "progress."[9] Even the pessimistic Williamson clarifies: "At the very least, we [philosophers] should learn from our mistakes, if only not to repeat them," and even if philosophy can be done in an armchair, there is no need to rush to the conclusion that "philosophy can nowhere usefully proceed until the experiments are done."[10] How to identify philosophical progress and whether philosophy contributes anything to the general store of knowledge are important questions, too, but to discuss them further here would distract me from exploring my initial question.

Up to this point, I have sought to illustrate some of the more general features characteristic of philosophy and to place us in a position to see why a person might be inclined to take up the fourth view. I began by raising the question of why academics and students might take the fourth view of philosophy (Philosophy has little or no influence on 99% of [insert discipline]). I offered a distinction between two orders of activity: doing and reflecting. I suggested that doing is typically to be done first and only after this reflecting.[11] Then I cited Lewis, Dennett and Williamson to the effect that philosophy treats what is already known and that this will bear upon what counts as philosophical progress and what philosophers

8. Lewis, *Mind and World Order*, 3.
9. Dummett, *Nature*.
10. Williamson, *Philosophy*, 6 and 22.

11. Many philosophers would likely respond in analogous ways. Lamont recounts talking with a philosopher teaching at Princeton who explained to her that most philosophers see their field as "superordinate" to other disciplines, and because of this every discipline at one point or other will have to submit their claims to philosophical analysis. See Lamont, *How Professors Think*.

might reasonably expect as a result of their philosophical efforts. Now let us consider how philosophy by virtue of being a second-order activity that reflects on first-order activities (what is already "known") contributes to the plausibility of the fourth view.

Philosophy has little to no influence on 99% of mathematics. In the context of the present discussion, one can interpret this to mean: 99% of mathematics (or whatever discipline) is not influenced by reflecting on the discipline or at least not influenced by reflecting in a way that qualifies as a second-order activity, once-removed from doing. One possible implication is that reflecting is not important to doing. Only *doing* is important to doing. Since *doing* is what we actually do in mathematics (or whatever discipline), there is very little need for refection. I think this insight is what people mean to express when they say 99% of what I do is not influenced by philosophy. Surely they will admit *some* kind of reflection is involved in doing. After all, it sounds absurd to say that mathematicians, for example, never reflect as they go about doing their mathematics. A rare combination of exacting yet playful reflection is characteristic of mathematical reasoning. It is an interesting mix of rigorous, abstract and creative thought processes. That said, it is widely held that the kind of reflection characteristic of philosophical reflection rarely takes place in mathematics.

Notwithstanding, when both Dummett and Williamson reflect upon the nature of philosophy, they do not hesitate to liken philosophy to mathematics. Dummett writes: "The example of mathematics benefits philosophy, despite their very different methodologies, by proving that thought, without any specialized input from experience, can advance knowledge in unexpected directions."[12] Williamson, too, compares philosophy to mathematics and considers mathematics to be like philosophy: "In practice, most of mathematics will and should remain an armchair discipline, even though it is not in principle insulated from experimental findings, because armchair methods, specifically proof, remain by far the most reliable and efficient available."[13] Yet insulation from "findings," as it were, is not enough to constitute an activity as a second-order activity—even if done from an armchair (i.e. with very little "doing"?). Otherwise, the fourth view would not be so popular among mathematicians (and other academicians). This

---

12. And also, interestingly enough, that "mathematics shares with philosophy a difficulty in saying what it is *about*." Dummett, *Nature*, 5.

13. Williamson, *Philosophy*, 7.

suggests that when philosophy is deemed irrelevant, sterile and self-indulgent, it is understood to be so in a way that mathematics is not.[14]

The main reason why the fourth view is so palatable among academics—and just because we are talking about philosophy here does not mean that philosophers aren't among them—is that, in many ways, it decries several intractable difficulties that beset us despite our best efforts of integrating different activities of first- and second- orders. For example, the way I would like to broach the first-order/second-order problem is to ask, what is the relationship between doing and reflecting? However, this innocuous question can hardly be asked without introducing a philosophical irony. For as far as I can see, it is questions like these that are responsible for the first- and second- order problematic in the first place. In other words, the very asking of these questions exacerbates the problem. The inquiry itself is already being undertaken in the context of reflection; however, at the same time, it constitutes a new *kind* of reflection, ostensibly reflecting upon reflecting and not upon doing. It is not at all clear how this new round of reflecting, a reflecting *twice*-removed (reflecting on reflecting on doing), will be able to say anything useful about second-order reflecting or its relationship to first-order activities. For example, I am inclined to examine reflecting's second-order relationship to first-order doing by examining it philosophically, but this removes me one step further from the problem under inspection. Not only this, but the more I try to elucidate matters (by asking more questions) it seems the further I extend my proximity to the first- and second- order dynamic. This is what I initially set out to investigate, but it illustrates, I think, a potentially gaping weakness of philosophy, at least from the perspective of doing. Once the decision is made to reflect, there is no non-arbitrary way to reign in inquisitive tendencies since the order of doing that would do so is already a reflecting.

Conversely, I find myself at a loss for compelling ways for getting doers to reflect at all. For example, Lockhart observes in mathematics how "rigorous formal proof only becomes important when there is a crisis—when you discover that your imaginary objects behave in a counterintuitive way; when there is a paradox of some kind." Otherwise, "it is the soul of mathematics to carry out [intuitive and informal] dialogue

---

14. Of course, it probably wouldn't be hard to find people who think that mathematics is irrelevant, sterile and self-indulgent. Yet philosophy, I bet they would say, is somehow thought to be more so.

with one's proof."[15] Yet the nature of proof is such that it "is completely self-contained; we're not awaiting any experimental confirmation."[16] This helps explain why Mycielski concluded above that if philosophy ever does manage to influence mathematics, it would have to restrict itself to the deciding of set theory's axioms. Furthermore, C. I. Lewis himself suggested that if common sense and philosophy always coincided, there would be no problems calling for philosophical attention. When Polya envisioned mathematics primarily as an extraordinary means of problem solving, he noted that all the heuristic procedures that practitioners routinely utilize are all "natural, simple, obvious, just plain common sense." He remarks: "The person who behaves the right way usually does not care to express his behavior in clear words and, possibly, he cannot express it so."[17] Whereas he himself sought clarity of expression, his advice to others was not to begin reflecting whenever a problem proved unsolvable, but rather "if you can't solve a problem, then there is an easier problem you can't solve: find it."[18] Lockhart counsels the same: "A good problem is something you don't know how to solve . . . A good problem does not just sit there in isolation, but serves as a springboard to other interesting questions."[19] And again:

> Mathematics is about problems, and problems must be made the focus of a student's mathematical life. Painful and creatively frustrating as it may be, students and their teachers should at all times be engaged in the process—having ideas, not having ideas, discovering patterns, making conjectures, constructing examples and counterexamples, devising arguments, and critiquing each other's work. Specific techniques and methods will arise naturally out of this process, as they did historically: not isolated from, but organically connected to, and an out-growth of, their problem-background.[20]

Thus, barring a crisis, there will rarely be a need or desire to transition from doing to reflecting. Moreover, the tried and true path to a deeper understanding of mathematics is simply more doing, not reflecting. If this

15. Lockhart, *Mathematician's Lament*, 72.
16. Lockhart, *Mathematician's Lament*, 118.
17. Polya, *How to Solve It*, 3.
18. Polya, *How to Solve It*, xxi.
19. Lockhart, *Mathematician's Lament*, 41.
20. Lockhart, *Mathematician's Lament*, 60–61.

is the case, then philosophy should count itself lucky for being able to influence mathematics at all (1% is better than 0%).

Unhappily (for philosophy), the fourth view seems to have considerable merit—at least when it comes to philosophy of mathematics. Why isn't philosophy's influence more widely felt? Why would a non-philosopher see philosophy as inconsequential to what he or she does? The reasons appear to involve the inability to integrate first- and second-order practices. One would expect philosophy to be able to do so, but philosophical attempts to do so will only exacerbate matters by introducing new problems involving the integration of second-order and higher order reflecting. How many disciplines are there that can repeat after mathematicians: "Philosophy has little or no influence on 99% of (insert discipline)"? I would say that depends. It seems to me that if a discipline has a vested interest in maintaining its intuitive self-understanding as a legitimate and identifiable research program, then philosophy may not be permitted to influence it at all, and that as a matter of principle. For as Rescher notes: "Procedural principles are in the end validated through the consideration of [their]utility and efficacy on the particular domain at practice that is at issue."[21]

Insofar as reflection is unable ultimately to contribute to what a discipline is doing, since the reflections themselves are endlessly open to further reflecting, philosophy instantly becomes (every?) discipline's undoing. In other words, what some disciplines do only in times of crisis philosophy appears to be in the habit of doing all the time. If philosophy by its very nature qualifies as a discipline in crisis, it is almost to be expected that the majority of disciplines will want little to nothing to do with it. The very attempt to integrate its reflective, anti-doing influence with any other factor, which itself would constitute reflecting, will contribute to the discipline's immediate un-doing. Thus, although certainly not telling the whole story, the fourth view of philosophy appears to be partially vindicated: Philosophy's un-doing effect should be kept at bay, allowing it to have little to zero influence on 99% of (insert discipline).[22]

---

21. Rescher, *Philosophical Dialectics*, 3.

22. This paper was presented at the annual meeting of the New Jersey Regional Philosophical Association, held at Bergen Community College, Paramus, New Jersey, November, 2010.

3

Some ideas on Husserl's remarks that mathematicians are not pure theoreticians

IN HIS *LOGICAL INVESTIGATIONS* (*Prol.* §71), Husserl states that mathematicians are not pure theoreticians but rather ingenious technicians and that the work of theoreticians falls to philosophers.[1] When he expounds on this idea in *The Crisis of European Science and Transcendental Phenomenology*, however, he senses that the *pathos* of his audience has changed. In *The Crisis*, he writes with apparent disillusionment over the continuing successes of mathematics, realizing that the prospect of enlisting them all for the service of phenomenology had grown considerably dimmer over time. Mathematicians—so it seemed to some at the time—were leaving philosophers with very little to do, and to someone like Husserl, this was a cultural indication of an underlying philosophical confusion. By way of response, Husserl reintroduces his programmatic question: what would it take for philosophy to become scientific? In this chapter, I briefly comment on Husserl's enigmatic remark—"the mathematician is not the pure theoretician but only the ingenious technician"—and provide in short compass an overview of the issues in philosophy of mathematics that likely prompted it.[2]

The task at hand is to try to contextualize Husserl's observation within the history and philosophy of mathematics. I will then make the suggestion that Husserl's phenomenological program qualifies as the work of an ingenious technician and not that of a pure theoretician.[3] For

---

1. "*Prol.* §" refers to a section of the Prologue of Husserl's *Logical Investigations*, vol. 1.

2. This claim is found in Husserl, *Logical Investigations*, 1.159.

3. In other words, the privileging of method persists. Rota claims philosophers take "the easy way out" if they conclude axiomatics is what makes mathematics unique. Compare Natorp: "If science—for [Husserl], as for Plato and Kant, already the same as mathematics—constructs theories, then philosophy enquires into the theory of theories."

any theory of "theories in general" remains a theory still and will, as a matter of course, eventually come to a place where it is made to reflect on itself.[4] When Husserl saw this happen in mathematics, he decried a transformation that was having the insidious effect of reducing pure science to sheer method. Yet for various reasons (and to his critics' increasing bewilderment), Husserl persisted with his own reductive project, thinking that phenomenology would not ultimately meet with the same fate.[5] Sebestik describes the Husserl of *Logical Investigations* as conducting an "ongoing search" where he maps out numerous possibilities but refuses to commit himself to any of them.[6] In our section (*Prol.* §71), Husserl is busy defending the far-reaching, formal achievements of mathematics and even encouraging their further expansion—which makes good procedural sense for Husserl, who always writes with ulterior, methodological aims in view. In this particular case, what Husserl appears to have in mind is the theoretical assimilation of the mathematics of his time with the overarching purposes of phenomenology.

Kline describes mathematics as confining itself to abstractions, specifically abstractions of numbers and geometric forms along with an assortment of concepts that constructively builds on these.[7] Interestingly, Husserl comes to see mathematics in a somewhat different light, as exemplified in the proclamation: "Only if one is ignorant of the modern science of mathematics, particularly formal mathematics, and measures it by the standards of Euclid or Adam Riese, can one remain stuck in the common prejudice that the essence of mathematics lies in number and

---

See Rota, "Ten Remarks," 92; Natorp, "Question of Logical Method," 39.

4. Rota emphasizes phenomenology's calling for rigorous, theoretical sciences (plural) appropriate to each of the individual sciences. My reading of Husserl agrees more with those who primarily see him as interested in devising a sort of fundamental "supertheory." In my view, Husserl suggests this can be achieved by conducting a series of reductions proceeding from physics to mathematics to logic to philosophy to phenomenology. Compare García Prado, "La fundamentación," 50–51. However, neither reading need exclude the other. "Even if it is not to be denied that in the *Prolegomena* the treatment of this logical technology serves the primary purpose of introducing pure logic as its theoretical foundation, one may nevertheless venture the assertion that Husserl's idea of a pure logic remains essentially bound to practical motives." See Bernet, Kern, and Marbach, *Introduction*, 28.

5. Tasić also casts Hilbert as one seeking a "mathematics of mathematics." See Tasić, *Mathematics*.

6. Sebestik, "Husserl," 59–60.

7. Kline, *Mathematics for the Nonmathematician*, 33.

quantity."[8] Lest anyone suppose Kline was ignorant of mathematics (!), I will attempt to contextualize Husserl's remark with respect to contemporary philosophy of mathematics.

The name Euclid is virtually synonymous with the Greek geometric tradition (i.e., "Euclidean geometry"). Irrespective of how much geometry Euclid actually produced, the compendium associated with his name (the *Elements*) so successfully consolidated ancient knowledge of plane geometry, geometric algebra, number theory and solid geometry that no other textbook is extant from that time period. According to Kline, "The impetus for the conception of a logical, mathematical approach to nature must be credited primarily to Euclid's *Elements*."[9] Yet according to Kline, it was not until the latter part of the nineteenth century that the search for mathematical design in nature ceased to be thought of as the search for truth.

Adam Riese (or Ries), by contrast, may seem an obscure name for Husserl to mention, particularly in the same breath as Euclid, but the persistence of the German phrase, "nach Adam Ries" ("according to Adam Ries"), provides evidence to the contrary.[10] While working as a municipal recorder of mine yields and mining shares in Annaburg, Germany, he ran a reputable school that used his own textbooks in mathematics. Due to high production costs, his algebra book never enjoyed wide circulation, but his books on arithmetic went through over one hundred editions between 1518 and 1656. He is best known for explaining multiple methods for calculating a vast number of computations. Vogel surmises that, "Ries did more than any previous author to spread knowledge of arithmetic."[11] In other words, Ries helped accomplish for arithmetic what Euclid achieved for geometry. Yet Vogel makes a remark, similar to Kline's, that "Ries failed to set forth the logical foundations of the subject. Instead, he simply presented formulas with the command 'Do it this way.'"[12]

Husserl perceives that the mathematics of his time should not be viewed merely as continuations of the Euclidean or Riesian projects. Before pursuing philosophy, Husserl did research in the calculus of variations,

---

8. Husserl, *Logical Investigations*, 1.159.
9. Kline, *Loss of Certainty*, 29.
10. Vogel, "Ries," 11.458.
11. Ibid.
12. Vogel, "Ries," 11.457.

Some ideas on Husserl's remarks

studying under such luminaries as L. Kronecker and K. Weierstrass.[13] Kronecker was persuaded that it was only proper for mathematicians to entertain those mathematical objects that actually exist. For example, natural numbers are instantiated everywhere in human experience, making these the best candidates for students to start with. His famous quip that "God created the integers, all else is the work of man" bespeaks the importance of invoking an axiom by fiat, allowing for the construction of numbers on the basis of already existing ones (e.g., "Let there be a Peano system").[14] But Kronecker was against mathematicians getting too carried away by creating fanciful "numbers." Among these, he counted irrationals, transcendentals, and infinite series. Limit-points, too, were famously off-limits.[15] The restrictions Kronecker had in mind in terms of what numbers were to be permitted seemed to Hilbert an impossible display of "ostrich-politics."[16] For not only was Kronecker effectively turning his back on issues at hand, he was ultimately, according to Hilbert, "throw[ing] the baby out with the bathwater."[17] The fallout of Kronecker's restrictions included a number of strained professional relationships, but more important for our purposes is the wholesale discounting of the cumulative accomplishment of Western mathematical history.[18] Denying irrational numbers, for example, would instantly bring mathematics "back to the state it had in Pythagoras's time."[19] Fortunately, most practitioners paid no heed to Kronecker's stricture (with Poincaré and Brouwer being notable exceptions).[20]

All the while, Weierstrass had been working on defining a curve that does not have a tangent at any point. For those outside the "Weierstrass school," this would come as somewhat of a shock. Intuition suggests that it is reasonable to expect some curves to lack tangents at "special" points,

13. Centrone, *Logic and Philosophy*.
14. Davis, "Number," 95.
15. See O'Connor and Robertson, "Kronecker."
16. Hilbert, "Extract," 2.944.
17. Ibid.
18. Edwards, "Kronecker's Place."
19. Maor, *Infinity and Beyond*, 65 n 7.
20. By identifying Kronecker as a "constructivist" and tacitly linking him to Husserl, Poincaré and Brouwer (and through them, Heidegger and Derrida), Tasić appears to be suggesting that Kronecker was one of many influences for the development of postmodern philosophy.

but the usual curves in calculus seem generally not to manifest this feature—or at least when they do, the domains can restrict to practically exclude (or at least deemphasize) these points. Weierstrass, however, was able to shatter this expectation by deliberately devising a curve that does not possess tangents at *any* point. While the prospect of such a curve is striking in itself, what proved revolutionary was the notion that mathematical intuitions cannot help practitioners "see" the curve. What Poincaré ended up calling a "monster function" was instantly recognized as a significant breakthrough by the broader mathematical community, for as Hahn makes clear, "only logical analysis can pursue this strange object to its final form."[21] The lesson learned was that for the first time mathematics has been proven to have the potential to go *beyond* intuition.

Husserl (*Prol.* §70) gives an account of what he sees as the difference between contemporary mathematics and all the mathematics that came before it:

> The *most general Idea of a Theory of Manifolds* is to be a science which definitely works out the form of the essential types of possible theories or fields of theory, and investigates their legal relations with one another. All actual theories are then specializations or singularizations of corresponding forms of theory, just as all theoretically worked-over fields of knowledge are *individual* manifolds. If the formal theory in question is actually worked out in the theory of manifolds, then all deductive theoretical work in constructing all actual theories of the same form has been done. This is a point of view of the highest methodological importance, without which there can be no talk of understanding the method of mathematics.[22]

If a theory is said to cover all instantiations of a specific sort, then as one inquires into the form of the theory, the form will identify features common to all theories of that sort. In this case, the *theory* in turn becomes the instantiation and anything worked out for that theory qua theory will also hold for all theories of that sort. Let us compare Husserl's remarks here with those of a contemporary mathematician who was working on similar problems within a different philosophical context.

---

21. Hahn, "Geometry," 186.
22. Husserl, *Logical Investigations*, 1.156.

Some ideas on Husserl's remarks

B. Russell brings together two observations that help elucidate what Husserl is attempting to convey. For example, Russell writes in the introduction to his *Introduction to Mathematical Philosophy*:

> It is clear that, if *formal* reasoning is what we are aiming at, we shall always arrive ultimately at statements like the above, in which no actual things or properties are mentioned; this will happen through the mere desire not to waste our time proving in a particular case what can be proved generally. It would be ridiculous to go through a long argument about Socrates, and then go through precisely the same argument again about Plato . . . Thus the absence of all mention of particular things or properties in logic or pure mathematics is a necessary result of the fact that this study is, as we say, "purely formal" (italics in original).[23]

But Russell goes on to explain in the introduction to the *Principia Mathematica*:

> Most mathematical investigation is concerned not with the analysis of the complete process of reasoning, but with the presentation of such an abstract of the proof as is sufficient to convince a properly instructed mind . . . [but] the investigations of Weierstrass and others of the same school have shown that, even in the common topics of mathematical thought, much more detail is necessary than previous generations of mathematicians had anticipated.[24]

One observation to make is that both Husserl and Russell are interested in the philosophy embedded in the practices of "formal" mathematics, "without which there can be no talk of understanding the method of mathematics." What both thinkers have come to appreciate is that much more consideration must be given to deciding what degree of rigor "is sufficient to convince a properly instructed mind." To help decide this, both agree that a better understanding of "logic" is programmatically crucial for making further progress.[25]

Without having to hedge our bets on a particular school of philosophy of mathematics, one can safely assert that what so impressed Husserl is the idea that "logic" can venture, if not beyond intuition, at least beyond

23. Russell, *Basic Writings*, 177.
24. Russell, *Basic Writings*, 163.
25. It is interesting that both, each in his own way, went on to wrestle with the prospect of completeness. Russell's Paradox is well known. For Husserl, see Hartimo, "Towards Completeness."

fundamental, but confused, pre-understandings.[26] Logic possesses the uncanny ability to reveal limitations in reasoning that intuition, left to itself, may never come to know. Husserl (*Prol.* §70) reflects Kronecker's insistence on the importance for mathematics of the construction of numbers. Its importance, however, does not lie in how certain numbers are of theoretical interest because they happen to "exist." Much rather, numbers are of special interest precisely because of the category "number" that the various kinds of numbers collectively make known. In the same way, geometry is crucial for understanding mathematics, but not because geometry can suggest to us a particular theory of space. The value of geometry derives from the category "geometry" that geometries (plural) seem to furnish cumulatively. Here we see why Husserl is motivated to speak of a "division of labor." There may be work for many kinds of "logicians" to do, be they mathematical, symbolic, or "pure." Yet the only one with a genuine interest in the "Idea" of a "theoretical science of theory in general" is the pure logician. For Husserl, then, there is no need to deny that mathematicians are brilliant technicians; it need only be kept in mind that *philosophers* are the only ones qualified to properly serve as theoreticians.

Even so, Husserl would never have considered *ancient* philosophers to be properly qualified. Husserl explains in *The Crisis* (Part 2, §8): "What is new, unprecedented, is the conceiving of this idea of a rational infinite totality of being with a rational science systematically mastering it . . . But this is not only in respect to ideal space. Even less could the ancients conceive of a similar but more general idea (arising from formalizing abstraction), that of a formal mathematics."[27] The culmination of this mathematical mindset is what Husserl identifies as "the completely new idea of *mathematical natural science*—Galilean science, as it was rightly called for a long time." According to Husserl (*The Crisis*, Part 2, §9, h), an unfortunate by-product of Galilean science is "the surreptitious substitution of the mathematically substructed world of idealities for the only real world, the one that is actually given through perception."[28] Mathematics, he claims, is the main catalyst for the Galilean transformation of science.

26. Tieszen comments that Husserl, though no platonist, is "also not a nominalist, factionalist, or strict Hilbertian formalist" and that he "disagrees with pragmatism and conventionalism about mathematics." See Tieszen, *Phenomenology*, 51.

27. Husserl, *Crisis*, 22.

28. Husserl, *Crisis*, 49.

Some ideas on Husserl's remarks

Regarding Galileo's popularity among philosophers, Finocchiaro once complained that he could think of no other scientist in history seized upon more by philosophers to bolster every kind of claim.[29] More recently, he singled out Husserl's *The Crisis* as a "classic instance."[30] Notwithstanding, Husserl sees Galileo as "the consummate discoverer," insisting "quite serious[ly]" that for a proper understanding of contemporary Western culture identifying Galileo at the "top of the list of the greatest discoverers of modern times" is critical.[31] Of interest for the present discussion is a diagram Galileo provides to help demonstrate that an infinite number of vacua can be contained in a finite space.[32] Comparing what Galileo insinuates about infinity via the use of this diagram with what Weierstrass describes as an everywhere-continuous-but-nowhere-differentiable function helps illustrate the point.

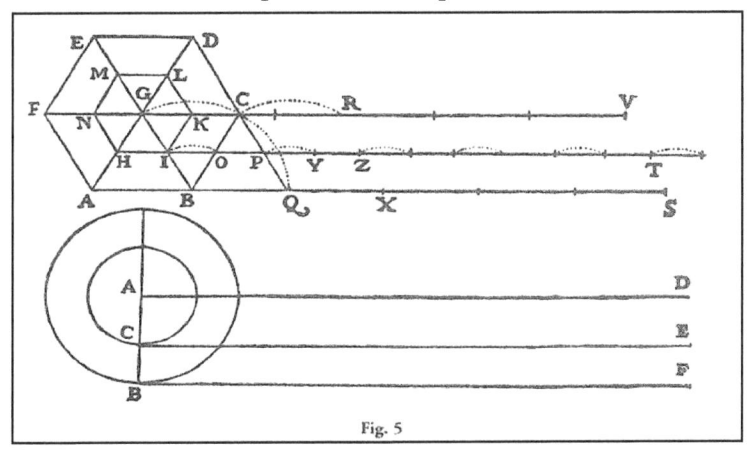

Fig. 5

29. Finocchiaro, "Galileo and Philosophy," 130. Similarly, Machamer mentions that a figure like Galileo is "full of interpretive fecundity," observing that "[p]hilosophically, Galileo has been used to exemplify many different themes, usually as a side bar to what the particular writer wished to make the hallmark of the scientific revolution or the nature of good science." See Machamer, "Galileo Galilei."

30. Finocchiaro, "Review of Dušan I. Bjelić," 755. When it comes to studying Galileo for doing philosophy, Finocchiaro reminds us of a need to distinguish philosophical reflections from historical accounts: "Philosophy ought not to be equated with either scholarship or history, however much one may love both." Perhaps this can also help temper Natorp's otherwise scathing critique: "Husserl has made an understanding of Kant impossible, an understanding which is so necessary for his purpose . . ." See Finocchiaro, "Philosophizing about Galileo," 258; Natorp, "Question of Logical Method," 241.

31. Galileo serves as a metonymy for all scientific developments of his time. Compare Kockelmans, "Mathematization," 52.

32. See Galileo, *Dialogues*.

Ideas at the Intersection of Mathmatics, Philosophy, and Theology

With the aid of a diagram (Fig. 5), Galileo compares the path traveled by two concentric hexagons with the path traveled by a pair of concentric circles as each is rolled along line segments of equal length.[33] The effectiveness of the diagram lies in how it enables readers to see both the beginning and end of Galileo's argument, quickly passing over an indefinite number of intermediate steps.[34] Beginning with a regular, six-sided polygon, readers are asked to increase the number of sides on their way to envisioning a regular, n-sided polygon where n continually approaches infinity. As the n-sided, regular polygon approaches an infinitely-sided, regular polygon, more and more "vacua," or "jumps," can be counted on the segment. Of particular interest is what is happening to the inside polygon. For the "more and more" of the inside polygon seems as if it should be greater than the "more and more" of the outside polygon. Galileo offers this example to help explicate what happens in the special case of circles, which were traditionally regarded as "polygons having an infinitude of sides." From this perspective, circles would exhibit an infinite number of points counterintuitively spanning a fixed and finite distance.[35] This scenario gives rise to a number of interesting conceptual puzzles.

For example, not only would it seem that the infinity corresponding to the smaller circle should be greater than the infinity corresponding to the larger (considering that they span congruent lines and given the former's smaller circumference), but the *sum* of the infinite points where the inside polygon touches the line and the infinite number of points where it "jumps" off the line is also contained on the line segment. Furthermore, there is the suggestion that the sum of the two infinites should be greater than either of the other two infinites when considered separately, and this in spite of an entrenched reluctance to entertain smaller and larger infinities.[36] What Galileo observes is that the infinity of points contained in the line segment incorporates both the infinity of sides of the given

---

33. Galileo, *Dialogues*, 16.

34. Compare Lubański's judgment: "From a *psychological* standpoint [Galileo's solution of the paradox] seems correct." See Lubański, "Galileo's View," 128

35. Galileo, *Dialogues*, 36. He muses: "may I not say . . . that when I have bent the straight line into a polygon having an infinite number of sides, i.e., into a circle, I have reduced to actuality that infinite number of parts which you claimed, while it was straight, were contained in it only potentially?"

36. Galileo, *Dialogues*, 29. Here he claims that it is a "serious error" to "discuss the infinite by assigning to it the same properties which we employ for the finite, the natures of the two having nothing in common."

polygon and the infinity of jumps for the given polygon. This prompts him to consider the notion of infinitesimals, particularly the role they might play in accounting for the continuum. In these and other ways, one hears echoes in Galileo's thinking of the same puzzling phenomena with which G. Cantor—a contemporary of Husserl and Weierstrass' most famous student—also sought to come to terms.[37]

In a sense, Galileo was fortunate enough to have recourse to diagrams; an inherited practice geometers accept as legitimate. By contrast, Weierstrass was not able to resort to diagrams, for there is no way to depict his final curve geometrically.[38] And this is precisely the point. According to Boyer, "neither [Cavalieri] nor Galileo appear to have been seriously interested in algebra, either as a manner of expression or as a form of demonstration."[39] Traditionally, mathematicians would only invoke infinity at the intermediate steps of geometric proofs, making sure ahead of time that the proper construction of the initial and final geometric forms was possible. Boyer clarifies: "It must be borne clearly in mind, however, that although the logical basis of the calculus is arithmetic, the new analysis resulted largely from suggestions drawn from geometry."[40] In the specific case of Galileo's paradoxes, an important contributing factor is an intuitive presumption: "there are no infinite circles, or infinite bodies at all."[41]

Yet as geometric shapes began to involve infinitesimals more and more and practitioners began translating them into algebraic expressions, George Berkeley wondered if any had thought to ask "whether such mathematicians as cry out against mysteries have ever examined their own principles."[42] He pondered why it had not occurred to math-

37. Parker sees Galileo, Bolzano, and Cantor as all wrestling with the same problems: "relations between numerosity and magnitude, the nature and structure of continua, and even physical applications." See Parker, "Philosophical Method," 94.

38. Hahn suggested a helpful series of diagrams to give an idea for what is happening:

See Hahn, "Geometry," 185.
39. Boyer, *History*, 121.
40. Boyer, *History*, 116.
41. Lubański, "Galileo's View," 132.
42. Berkeley, "Berkeley's Criticisms," 557.

ematicians to give an account of the infinitesimal calculus: "For when it is said, let the increments vanish, i.e. let the increments be nothing, or let there be no increments, the former supposition that the increments were something, or that there were increments, is destroyed, and yet a consequence of that supposition, i.e. an expression got by virtue thereof, is retained."[43] Thus a perceived need grew for the establishing by rigor of what over time had become a matter of accepted practice. New methods were sought to attempt to meet this need, but in Husserl's view (*The Crisis*, Part 2, §9, k), "the progressive fulfillment of the task" somehow managed to lose the "originally vital consciousness of the task which gives rise to the methods."[44] Hence Husserl's judgment: "In his actual sphere of inquiry and discovery [the mathematician] does not know at all that everything these reflections must clarify is even in *need* of clarification."[45] In this way, the mathematician remains "at best a highly brilliant technician of the method."[46]

Thus even a consideration of how to properly justify geometers' appeals to constructions leads to theoretical difficulties. According to Husserl (*Logical Investigations*, II §20), diagrams are properly thought of as "Ideas" and abstraction is most adequately construed as "a peculiar consciousness which, on an intuitive basis, directly apprehends a Specific Unity." However, when a series of developments in abstraction results in a chain of successive reductions (from geometry to arithmetic, arithmetic to algebra, algebra to symbolic systems which are entirely devoid of meaning), serious problems arise for Husserl.[47] Methods initially created for *specific, historical* purposes—"idealization, formalization, and functionalization"—cease to be understood as such, becoming instead mistaken for "independent and self-sufficient entities."[48]

Yet for all the effort he exerts continually identifying and clarifying these themes, the work in which Husserl engages somehow seems always only just preliminary. Writing as early as 1917, Chandler recognized similarities between the all-encompassing project of Husserl and

43. Berkeley, "Berkeley's Criticisms," 556.
44. Husserl, *Crisis*, 56.
45. Husserl, *Crisis*, 57.
46. Husserl, *Crisis*, 56.
47. Which I sought to help illustrate by comparing Galileo and Weierstrass.
48. Kockelmans, "Mathematization," 62.

that proposed earlier by Kant: "When Kant said that we can learn philosophizing but not philosophy, he betrayed the unscientific character of philosophy."[49] Initially, Husserl hoped to help remedy this by picking up where Kant had left off, but his meta-philosophical focus had to turn back on itself eventually and, once this happened, perpetually contemplate method. Chandler observes that Husserl had little to show for himself insofar as promising to "lift philosophy above the plane of conflicts."[50] Now, nearly a century later, philosophy remains pluralistic as ever, and the phenomenological approach is considered one among many. Yet in hindsight this is what Husserl should have expected, particularly given what was happening in the history and philosophy of mathematics.[51]

For example, in a paper on irrational numbers, Dedekind conceded, "Even now such resort to geometric intuition in a first presentation of the differential calculus, I regard as exceedingly useful, from the didactic standpoint, and indeed indispensible, if one does not wish to lose too much time. But that this form of introduction into the differential calculus can make no claim to being scientific, no one will deny."[52] To bridge the gulf between practice and theory is rarely an easy task. For his part, Dedekind established a requirement that "arithmetic shall be developed out of itself." Every procedural rule posits definitions and typically relies on "common notions," but what are these "common notions" if not based in mathematical intuition? Parker points to a pluralistic case involving Galileo and Cantor, specifically their different decisions in accepting either one or both of the following common notions: "The whole is greater than its part" and "Two collections are equal in numerosity if and only if their members can be put in one-to-one correspondence."[53] The systems that result differ, depending on the acceptance or rejection of the first common notion.

---

49. Chandler, "Husserl's Program," 638.

50. Chandler, "Husserl's Program," 648.

51. Even in disciplines where phenomenology seems to have the best chance of contributing, there have been calls for theoretical pluralism. Compare Chemero, *Cognitive Science*, 16.

52. Dedekind, "Dedekind on Irrational Numbers," 573.

53. Parker, "Philosophical Method," 89–90. Parker calls these "Euclid's Principle" and "Hume's Principle" respectively. Compare DeMorgan: "If A and B can be correlated in 1—1 fashion then A cannot be a subset of B and B cannot be a subset of A." See Sagal, "Peirce on Infinitesimals," 133.

An analogous case of pluralism involves the conception of the continuum. Cantor demonstrated how the aggregate of all real numbers can be characterized by saying 1) it is an aggregate that is dense in itself and closed; 2) it contains as part all the rational numbers; and 3) between any two elements x_0 and x_1, other rational numbers lie. But after accepting this, questions still come to mind: do the real numbers characterize a geometric one-dimensional line "in an exhaustive manner"?[54] Or perhaps putting it another way: "Which is the *real* real number line?"[55] C. Peirce, for example, refused arithmetic as an adequate model for the continuum, preferring to approach the idea topologically.[56] According to Peirce, a more fruitful intuition of the continuum conceives it as a line in 2-space "where we cannot get from one side to the other, using smooth motion and by staying on the two dimensional surface."[57] Incidentally, a form of "nonstandard" analysis has now been rigorously developed, which makes full use of infinitesimals (the notion Weierstrass hoped to replace with his δ-ε method for limits). Observers remark that the content of some results in nonstandard analysis prove *less* clear when translated to standard terminology.[58] Surely, this would not have surprised Peirce. In fact, he might even have anticipated practitioners eventually coming across results refusing to be translated at all.

What Husserl was trying to capture for philosophy was the way mathematics had become a trustworthy science for the "development of form from fact."[59] If Bourbaki could describe mathematics as the study of "mother structures,"[60] Husserl conceived philosophical investigation as studying the structure of structure. But even mathematics evinces various degrees of pluralism: how much more unwieldy would philosophy's "logic" turn out to be! In fact, H. Smart was even doubtful that Husserl's

54. Cantor claimed that the properties of the real numbers characterize the continuum "in an exhaustive manner." See Cantor, "Contributions," 1165 (§11).

55. Sagal, "Peirce," 134.

56. Peirce explains: "A perfectly satisfactory logical account of the conception of continuity is required. This involves the definition of a certain kind of infinity, and in order to make that quite clear, it is requisite to begin by developing the logical doctrine of infinite multitude. This doctrine still remains, after the works of Cantor, Dedekind, and others, in an inchoate condition." See Dauben, "Philosophy of Infinite," 128.

57. Herron, "Theories of Infinitesimals," 608.

58. See Insall and Weisstein, "Nonstandard Analysis."

59. Mac Lane, *Mathematics*, 6.

60. Mac Lane, *Mathematics*, 7.

phenomenology could yield any insight that had not already been attained via other existing philosophies.[61] Commenting on Husserl's philosophy, he went on to lament: "[Husserl's] contribution remains a program to the very end."[62]

Phenomenology has grown as a movement to encompass a distinct set of methods (or "attitudes") and has not failed to produce a steady line of technicians, but not theoreticians.[63] Perhaps this can be helpfully illustrated by way of the following comparison. Reflecting on what "logicism" has accomplished since the time of Frege and Dedekind, Wagner judges that logicism was only half correct, for it got the mathematics right but the philosophy wrong.[64] Given developments in modern mathematics, some of which were described above, Husserl bequeathed to phenomenology his own programmatic search for a pure and scientific "logic." But just like logicism, his instincts seem to have proven only half correct. He got things right insofar as his unrelenting queries sought to better appreciate what philosophy might stand to learn from reflecting on mathematics. Yet he was wrong to surmise that this should ultimately be done for the sake of making philosophy scientific. Phenomenology seems much rather to have provided philosophy with fresh and creative ways for making meta-science more perspectival, which has lead, interestingly enough, to mutual enrichments both in psychology and cognitive science, but less so in philosophy and, least of all, in mathematics.[65]

---

61. See Smart, "Predicament."

62. Smart, "Predicament," 599.

63. Which raises the question, as it did for Kant, of whether "pure theory" is something we can pursue at all. For contemporary uses of phenomenological methods in psychology and cognitive science, see Thompson, *Mind in Life*.

64. Wagner, "Logicism," 65.

65. Gallagher and Zahavi go so far as to proclaim: "[A]ny contemporary introduction to the cognitive sciences should include a substantial discussion of phenomenology." Even Chandler begrudgingly admitted: "The only novelty it can claim is that of emphasizing a somewhat neglected aspect of psychology." See Gallagher and Zahavi, *Phenomenological Mind*, 217; Chandler, "Husserl's Program," 646. This paper was prepared for a conference at the Franciscan University of Steubenville on "Early Phenomenology," in April 2011.

4

Some ideas on Heidegger and the influence of mathematics and science on metaphysics

IN WHAT FOLLOWS, I offer reflections on Heidegger's lecture, "What is Metaphysics?" I am specifically interested in what role his curious mention of "the nothing" plays in his conception of metaphysics and how his short discussion of "truth" in *Being and Time*, idiosyncratically contributes to this conception. Taking his lead from Husserl, his teacher, Heidegger seems intent on contrasting his own preoccupation with ontology with stereotypical, analytic approaches to philosophy of mathematics, conflating these with popular views regarding science and mathematics as disciplines.

Despite recent efforts made by D. Zimmerman, T. Sider and others, contemporary intellectual culture does not yet seem ready to give metaphysics a full hearing. As C. I. Lewis quipped nearly a century ago, "Metaphysics has always been the dumping ground for problems that are only partly philosophic."[1] In some quarters, one might be reluctant to even use the word unless by "metaphysics" one means to say (winking her eye), "fundamental ontology" or "philosophy *after* metaphysics." Ever since Kant's Copernican Revolution (and perhaps even before then), metaphysics has fallen out of vogue in the "post-Kantian" West. Heidegger's writings and lectures have been influential participants in this trend. According to Heidegger, philosophy should seek to do away with metaphysics, or at the very least, radically re-conceive it with more authenticity. In many ways, Heidegger can be considered exemplary of the "continental" attitude toward metaphysics.

---

1. Lewis, *Mind and World Order*, 4.

Some ideas on Heidegger

It is interesting to note that at the outset of "What is Metaphysics?" (1929) Heidegger does not even bother to define the discipline or to discuss what kinds of investigations the discipline traditionally has involved.[2] Rather than define metaphysics, he is content to have it "introduce itself." In his discussion of the "unfolding" of metaphysics—which, he claims, is the only proper way to investigate *the* metaphysical question— Heidegger suggests two essential properties of metaphysical questions: 1) metaphysical questions will always treat the whole of metaphysics, and 2) metaphysical questions can only be asked in ways that have the questioner participating in the question. Only then can metaphysics genuinely "introduce itself."

Heidegger develops this further in *Introduction to Metaphysics* (an essay based on a 1935 lecture—six short years after the "What is Metaphysics?" lectures):

> To state the interrogative sentence, even in a tone of questioning, is not yet to question. To repeat the interrogative sentence several times in succession does not necessarily breathe life into the questioning; on the contrary, saying the sentence over and over may well dull the questioning. . . . Merely to have information, however abundant is not to know. . . . But to know means: to be able to stand in the truth.[3]

That not everyone has been able to do this is one inference to draw,[4] but a bolder claim seems to be that metaphysicians—up through and including Heidegger's own time—have not been in the habit of doing metaphysics at all. The reason philosophers have not been able to obtain "knowledge" is because for all their philosophical musing they have not been able to "question" effectively. It would appear that the advent of modern science has distracted philosophers from questioning.

In Heidegger's view, modern science may seem an impressive discipline, but it really should not be considered any more impressive than any other field, for all disciplines metaphysically operate on an even playing field. Not even mathematics is positioned to over-impress since a discipline's "exactness" is not to be confused with its existential "rigor." Indeed,

---

2. Ibid. According to C. I. Lewis, for example, "Metaphysics studies the nature of reality in general."

3. Heidegger, *Introduction to Metaphysics*, 17.

4. Contrast C. I. Lewis who insists that *everyone* can and should do philosophy.

in terms of rigor, philosophy (and this would hold for any other discipline) can be shown to stack up just as well.[5] In his judgment, Western culture is now so metaphysically confused that it has become incapable of distinguishing rigor from exactness. An unreasonable expectation persists in the Western mind such that any "serious" discipline should exhibit an exactness impossible for all but the natural sciences. Western culture is oblivious to the fact that non-science fields are just as rigorous *since the scientists who do science live in this world.*[6]

Whether scientific or not, Western intellectual culture blissfully exhibits the "hardened forgetfulness of being." In Heidegger's view, scientists have forgotten all about being. "Relation to the world," "attitude," and "irruption" are among the things that the history of Western thought has—from the beginning—turned a blind eye toward. Most tragically, the "Dasein"—or "being there"—has been forgotten out of mind, in spite of the truth that "being there" in the world is the very condition that makes it possible for metaphysics to introduce itself.

Heidegger chides scientists for not purposively attending to what he sees as the most important metaphysical question of all, the question of being. According to Heidegger (and he is not alone—his teacher Husserl, for example, seemed convinced of this), the fact that science has historically worked out its own disciplinary boundaries in the exclusionary ways that it has is to be blamed on the Western metaphysical tradition stemming from Plato to Kant.[7] Scientists may presume that they know about being, but that does not negate the fact that they do not know it at all, *for if they did*, according to Heidegger, then they would know about "the nothing," which scientists dismiss procedurally out of hand. He chides the tradition by observing: "Ultimately this is the scientifically rigorous

---

5. Here Heidegger may be alluding to and agreeing with Husserl's opening remarks in "Philosophy as Rigorous Science." Eventually, he set himself against the main contours of Husserl's proposed course of investigation.

6. Once again, compare C. I. Lewis, who insists that scientists do not "just report the facts."

7. Curiously, Descartes takes the brunt of Heidegger's attack. Some writers observe Heidegger is merely parroting Nietzsche. Elden, for his part, suggests that "Heidegger wants to free 'space' (*Raum*) from the Cartesian understanding, where it is based on the notion of extension." Faye more ominously links Heidegger's critique of Descartes to his growing sympathies for Nazism. See Elden, "Place of Geometry," 312; Faye, *Heidegger*, 15–16.

Some ideas on Heidegger

conception of the nothing. We know it, the nothing, in that we wish to know nothing about it."[8]

Working at the foundations of science and mathematics, one will encounter philosopher-logicians. C. Hartshorne expresses the conviction of many of these thinkers when he remarks that logic is the "backbone of philosophy" and that "nothing is quite clear logically until it can be put mathematically."[9] That Heidegger was in actual conversation with philosophers such as Bertrand Russell and Alfred Jules Ayer may or may not have been the case. Nevertheless, together, "What is Metaphysics?" and *Introduction to Metaphysics* mount an impressive, existential pushback against logico-mathematical styles of doing philosophy. Today, in analytic circles, the thrust of Heidegger's complaint might take a different form. For example, A. Vaidya makes the sensible point that decisions regarding *which* logic to use rest on foundationally metaphysical principles.[10] However, at the time of Heidegger's writing Russell and other logicists were adamant in their claims that all human knowledge can be reduced to logic. To help achieve this goal, Ayer and those associated with the Vienna Circle came to disdain all non-"positivistic" philosophy, which quickly came to include any metaphysical statement that could not be further reduced to a minimal cluster of clearly articulated, logical "givens."[11] In their view, the goal of philosophy was to pattern all human thought after logic. Indeed, so confident were they in the potential of this new approach that some (such as Carnap) were expectant to uncover the "Logical Structure of the World" (published by Carnap, incidentally, in 1928). From one vantage, at least, Heidegger might be interpreted as desperately, if not helplessly, rebelling against these and like-minded traditions when he insists that "no amount of scientific rigor attains to the seriousness of metaphysics."[12] It is not so much that logical assertions are wrong but that they do not do justice to the human world they purport to describe.[13]

---

8. Heidegger, "What is Metaphysics?" 98.

9. Hartshorne, *Creative Synthesis*, xvii.

10. Vaidya, "Metaphysical Foundation," 179–182.

11. Pincock explains that the aim of Carnap's *Aufbau*, for example, is "to provide a constitution system in which all scientific objects are constituted out of a few in a fully rigorous logical way." See Pincock, "Carnap's Logical Structure," 952.

12. Compare Dahlstrom, *Heidegger's Concept*, 23.

13. Compare Dreyfus, *Being-in-the-World*, 212–213.

In "What is Metaphysics?" Heidegger claims that among and with everything we sensually experience, there still remains *something else*, something that we can sense and that he fatefully decides to call "the nothing." One can feel the nothing lurking in the things that are; we must strike up the nerve, therefore, to talk about it, that is, *if* philosophers are going to really be rigorous and relate in authenticity to what is. Yet here logic is no help whatsoever, he claims, because if we adhere strictly to the dictates of logic, we cannot discuss the nothing at all.

Heidegger formulates the following line of reasoning: In order to talk about the nothing, we have to consider it as something, yet if we consider it as something, it would no longer be nothing, but something, which is absurd. Nothing is nothing and not something. Still, in order to examine nothing, we need to change nothing into something, which means we actually investigate something else, namely, the *concept* of nothing. The concept of nothing is not nothing, but something; therefore, "logic," as Heidegger calls it, has no place for nothing. *But Heidegger has a place for the nothing.* He insists that the nothing must be acknowledged and if that requires adopting tools for exploration other than mathematics and logic, then so be it. There is debate over whether on account of this argument Heidegger's thought succumbs to "irrationality." Carnap was among the first to inveigh such a charge against him. Wilberg explains:

> For it requires only a little rational reconstruction of Carnap's position to see that on his view the two uses of the word 'nothing' he discusses—negative existential quantification on the one hand and reference to an entity on the other—jointly exhaust the legitimate usage of the word, essentially because these are the only uses that are formalizable using predicate logic. So the fact that Heidegger is trying to use the word in some mysterious third way, far from constituting a rebuttal of Carnap's case, is rather precisely what indicts him on Carnap's view.[14]

Heidegger's own suggestions involve the existential investigation of the nothing through fits of joy, boredom and despair. Since Dasein *is* "being-there" in despair and anxiety, it is already "being held out into the nothing," a state of affairs that Western metaphysics has yet to fully appreciate. It is not difficult to see just how sharply Heidegger hoped to distinguish his philosophical enterprise from the pursuits of the likes of

---

14. See Wilberg, "Review of Heidegger."

scientists and mathematicians (or at least, philosophers who began to see philosophy as an extension of science and mathematics). As Glazebrook comments, for Heidegger, "[t]he route to ontology is the thoughtful recognition of its preclusion by the sciences."[15] In contradistinction to science and mathematics, Heidegger's Dasein is conceived as intrinsically and constitutionally involved with what disciplines such as these methodologically exclude.

In his book, *Being and Time*, Heidegger expands upon his initial thoughts on the nothing. By this time, he has begun to search out more systematically what the shortcomings of philosophy are in terms of its historical development.[16] Particularly striking are Heidegger's comments that it should not be a matter of consternation that the reality of the Real cannot be proven to everyone's satisfaction. In his view, a more pressing problem is: "Why Dasein as being-in-the-world has the tendency of 'initially' burying the 'external world' in nullity 'epistemologically' in order first to prove it."[17] What Heidegger refers to as "the external world" has been hidden by philosophers, but we might yet count it an "initial" hiding since at any time the possibility for its recovery still remains. In fact, what is buried *must* be recovered, writes Heidegger, but proofs will not suffice for this task: the prospect of recovery lies elsewhere. Central to recovery is the notion of "Dasein being-in-the-world." This way of understanding the human condition "is distinguished in principle from all realism in that realism believes that the reality of the 'world' needs proof, and at the same time is capable of proof."[18] The implication is not so much that philosophy cannot live up to its empirical/deductive ideals (a paradigm imported from scientific and/or mathematical inquiry), but merely that philosophy becomes immeasurably impoverished whenever it is made to do so.

The nothing, then, is an explicitly *ontological* problem that logic cannot properly assimilate. The problem is not, then, strictly logical or even strictly epistemological.[19] The audacious claim being made is that

---

15. Glazebrook, *Heidegger's Philosophy*, 131.

16 Compare Steiner, who also sees a connection between Heidegger's mention of "the nothing" in "What is Metaphysics?" and his discussion of truth in *Being and Time*. See Steiner, *Martin Heidegger*, 114–116.

17. Heidegger, *Being and Time*, 191.

18. Heidegger, *Being and Time*, 192.

19. According to Stone, both Heidegger and his critic, Carnap, were responding to

the problem has yet to be articulated by any other philosopher in the history of the Western tradition, which prompts the question: "Why should this not be a legitimate question?" The question he has in mind is this: "*How is the relation between an ideal being and a real thing objectively present to be grasped ontologically?*" Logic and epistemology have had their way with philosophy long enough. They have imported into philosophy a "scientific" attitude that is entirely misplaced. Once this was accomplished, the paramount question within metaphysics became ignored. Thus Heidegger asks, "[A]re we not allowed to ask about the ontological meaning of the relation between the real and the ideal?"[20]

In *Being and Time*, Heidegger seems convinced that if his existential conception of truth can be shown to be more "primordial" than the traditional, correspondence conception of truth, then he will have an occasion to suggest that traditional notions of truth are inferior since they are derivative to his. To establish truth, for Heidegger, is to demonstrate "not an agreement of knowing with its object, still less something psychical with something physical, but neither is it an agreement between the 'contents of consciousness' among themselves." Rather, "What is to be demonstrated is solely the being-discovered of the being itself, *that being* in the how of its being discovered. . . ." which "is ontologically possible only on the basis of being-in-the-world."[21] In short, "[b]eing true as discovering is a manner of being of Dasein," and "[d]iscovering is a way of being of being-in-the-world."[22]

Heidegger's aim is to emphasize the being of Dasein as essentially constituted as a "thrown project." Dasein is "thrown" into a definite world, in possession of its own potentiality of being: "'There is' being—not beings—only insofar as truth is. And truth *is* only because and as long as Dasein is."[23] By playing down the descriptive adequacy of propositional logic and setting aside the coherence of propositional systems, Heidegger finds opportunity to remark that a "skeptic can no more be refuted than the being of truth can ever be "proved." If the skeptic "has obliterated Dasein," she "does *not even need* to be refuted" since "Dasein cannot first

---

Husserl's phenomenological subsuming of "pre-Kantian metaphysics within the framework of Kantian epistemology." See Stone, "Heidegger and Carnap," 217.

20. Heidegger, *Being and Time*, 200.
21. Heidegger, *Being and Time*, 201.
22. Heidegger, *Being and Time*, 201, 202.
23. Heidegger, *Being and Time*, 211.

be subjected to proof for its own part."[24] Truth and falsity, proof and refutation, these are all existentially subordinate to the "disclosedness" and "discovery" of Dasein with the former being dependent on the latter for their very intelligibility.

With an "existentially conceived kind of being of truth," Heidegger posits that "truth . . . *is a kind of being of Dasein.*" The problem with abstract, correspondence theories of truth is that they can easily "be removed from the arbitrariness of Dasein." Moreover, all such theories only become intelligible *by virtue of Dasein*, "a being that is concerned in its being about its own most potentiality-of-being."[25] This observation is very important to Heidegger. Propositions, proofs, truth-judgments, all these are subsequent concerns; they cannot presuppose the existentially conceived being of truth. By re-conceiving truth, Heidegger renders science and mathematics inadequate to the task of pursuing original truth. It simply is not the case that when someone makes a judgment, truth is *necessarily* presupposed. On the contrary, "truth is already presupposed even when no one is *judging*, insofar as Dasein is at all."[26] Once again, Heidegger's Dasein is deliberately conceived so that it becomes a kind of necessary condition for science and mathematics to operate at all.

The nothing is not mere negation, a counterpoint to being for strictly logical purposes. The nothing offers subtle insights into the essence of being. In fact, the "thrownness" of being is primarily experienced when Dasein *encounters* the nothing. The problem is that science dismisses the nothing with "a lordly wave of the hand," but the nothing does not thereby automatically disappear.[27] Heidegger goes so far as to say that scientists, mathematicians, and contemporary philosophers authentically do what they have never actually done even when they *think* they have been doing it all along: the primordial nature of existence persists even though it has been ignored in the West since the beginning. The neglect of which Heidegger speaks is symptomatic of developments in philosophy and the disciplines of modern science and mathematics, for they have not only

24. Heidegger, *Being and Time*, 210.
25. Heidegger, *Being and Time*, 208, 209.
26. Heidegger, *Being and Time*, 210.
27. What the nothing "does" exactly is unclear. Compare Grene: "Such word-play may, indeed, be pretentious, vicious, or just silly. Heidegger's often is any or all of these. There is of course the famous case of 'nothing noths,' which may or may not be nonsense; I don't know." See Grene, *Philosophy*, 30.

obscured the phenomenological meaning of being but also the possibility of fruitfully inquiring after *the question* of the meaning of being: "As an attitude adopted by a being, the questioner, questioning has its own character of being... But already when we ask, 'What is "being?"' we stand in an understanding of the 'is' without being able to determine conceptually what the 'is' means."[28] *This* kind of investigation requires an existential procedure substantially different from the typical philosophical inquiry that marks Western philosophical tradition. "Logic with its categories would come too late; it could only negate after the fact, but it could never conceptualize 'the more original' prevailing of the 'Nothing,' which makes this 'no' possible and which dread experiences."[29]

Reminiscent of Husserl, Heidegger laments that science, mathematics, and even philosophy have programmatically relinquished their ability to provide answers to the question of the meaning of being.[30] To him, "the thrownness of being there"—"Dasein's being-in-the-world"—is the only consideration that can allow metaphysics to introduce itself and position truth to become enlivened. Heidegger seeks an existential remedy for the lack of vision characteristic of early twentieth-century metaphysics, a symptom of which is its methodological conception of philosophy as primarily a logico-mathematical pursuit.

According to E. J. Squires, "the task of science is to explain human experience. The concept of experience is there at the outset; without it there is nothing for science to be about."[31] "Our aim is to explain experience; to tell a convincing story about what is actually happening 'out there.' Certainly if we give up looking for explanations we will not find them, so some of us, at least, will continue to try."[32] "Philosophy," on the other hand (and now turning to a quote from Heidegger), "gets under way only by a peculiar insertion of our own existence into the fundamental possibilities of Dasein as a whole."[33] Human experience may be a basic aspect of both enterprises, but Heidegger sets philosophy apart by asking, "have we not

---

28. Heidegger, *Being and Time*, 4.
29. Marx, *Heidegger and the Tradition*, 95.
30. Different writers find different "sources" for Heidegger's thought. For an interpretation of Heidegger as carrying out an essentially Husserlian project, see Moran, "Heidegger's Transcendental."
31. Squires, "Quantum Theory," 92.
32. Squires, "Quantum Theory," 95.
33. Heidegger, "What is Metaphysics?"

already come to the end of our inquiry into the nothing—assuming that . . . 'logic' is of supreme importance, that the intellect is the means, and thought the way, to conceive the nothing originally and to decide about its possible exposure?" Heidegger's primary focus is on the "insertion" of the philosopher—the very being who is *doing* the questioning—into a complicated mix of beings where abounding, existential possibilities await. Where logic does not dare to tread, Heidegger might say, despair and anxiety—indeed, *angst*—can succeed.

In *Being and Time*, Heidegger writes: "Newton's laws, the law on contradiction, and any truth whatsoever, are true only as long as Dasein *is*. Before there was any Dasein, there was no truth; nor will there be any after Dasein is no more." This does not mean to say that "the beings which [Newton's laws] point out in a discovering way did not previously exist" even if "[b]efore Newton's laws were discovered, they were not 'true.'"[34] Rather the laws "became true through Newton, through them beings in themselves became accessible for Dasein." The insertion of the questioner into the world of beings is what matters: this is where the full gamut of existential possibility awaits her. Truth is the fundamental way for Dasein to have its being in the world. Science and mathematics have their place to be sure, yet his polemics against science and mathematics—indeed the whole of Western metaphysics—seem to be in danger of undercutting the impetus that gave rise to these disciplines in the first place.

There is more than one way to fend off logicism, however. A generation earlier, the French mathematician Henri Poincaré (1854-1912) had made the following points: "This science [mathematics] does not have for its unique objective to eternally contemplate its own navel; it touches nature and some day it will make contact with it. On this day it will be necessary to discard the purely verbal definitions and not any more be the dupe of empty words . . ."[35] Poincaré broaches some of Heidegger's concerns, perhaps in a way more conducive than the latter to the practice of scientific inquiry. The creation of mathematical models that "fit" the real world so well might lead one to conclude that 1) there is more than logic driving science in general and mathematics in particular; and 2) there is a profound connection between scientists' and mathematicians' conscious experiences and intuitions and the structure of the world they

34. Heidegger, *Being and Time*, 208.
35. Cited in Kline, *Loss of Certainty*, 227.

culturally inhabit. Since the time of Heidegger's writing, mathematical logicism has been more or less discredited, but the relationship between human consciousness and the mathematical structures of reality might still be a topic of interest.

According to Dummett, the logicists were "defeated by the problem of mathematical objects because they had incompatible aims." The composite problem of connecting human consciousness to the mathematical structure of the world ultimately foiled the logicist agenda because it sought "to represent mathematics as a genuine science, that is, as a body of *truths*, and not a mere auxiliary of other sciences; to keep it uncontaminated from empirical notions; and to justify classical mathematics in its entirety, and, in particular, the untrammeled use of classical logic in mathematical proofs."[36] Heidegger's decision to subsume modern science, mathematics and philosophy into a single cultural construct, "the Western tradition," and to show the shortcomings of "logic" for describing the world of Dasein obscures the reality of methodological (and ideological) pluralism in Western thinking.

Further, it lumps together the many disciplines as if they all shared the same ethos. Dummett points out, for example, that "there is nothing in mathematics that could be described as inference to the best explanation,"[37] which sets mathematics fundamentally apart from both scientific and philosophical practice. There are other factors as well that are operative in each of these three disciplines: aesthetics, creativity and serviceability, to name a few. Quine proposed five "benefits" gained by the adoption of our fruitful theories: simplicity, familiarity of principle, scope, fecundity, and successful results when tested.[38] Yet mathematicians are not always concerned with whether mathematical constructs can account for empirical facts, which opens up a theoretical space, I would think, where one might begin to address Heidegger's existential problematic.

How is it that mathematics can be made to fit the world? Cannot mathematics be made to partially describe the nothing even as it methodologically occludes its "lurking"? Can mathematics be said to already

---

36. Dummett, "What is Mathematics?" 26. But see Field's argument that aside from empirical knowledge, "the rest of the knowledge that separates those who know lots of mathematics from those who know only a little is knowledge of a purely logical sort." See Field, "Mathematical Knowledge."

37. Dummett, "What is Mathematics?" 13.

38. Quine, *Ways of Paradox*, 247.

be in the truth? How does one distinguish the mathematical from the empirical?[39] These and other questions all seem to touch on Heidegger's concerns, yet they are inherited from the history of traditional metaphysics as well as the history of philosophy of mathematics.

It is no secret that Husserl became critical of Heidegger for degenerating his vision of transcendental phenomenology into (what seemed to him) a thoroughly historical anthropology. Even so, it is with an anthropological interpretation of mathematics that I would like to conclude this short paper:

> Men like G. H. Hardy [an English mathematician (1847-1947)], who know, through their own experience as well as from the observation of others, that mathematical realities enter the mind from the outside, understandably—but erroneously—conclude that they have their origin and locus in the external world, independent of man. Erroneous, because the alternative to "outside the human mind," the individual mind, that is, is not "the external world, independent of man," but culture, the body of traditional thought and behavior of the human species.[40]

Would not Heidegger most certainly agree with this? Yet as far as I can see, this is one of the key tenets of American pragmatism. In the end, I agree with Hartshorne's comparative assessment: Heidegger's points are, on the whole, more compellingly expressed by pragmatists.[41] An anthropological approach like Heidegger's can still prove insightful if "[m]athematical realities thus have an existence independent of the individual mind, but are wholly dependent upon the mind of the species."[42] But has this not more helpfully been communicated by C. S. Peirce and C. I. Lewis, for example?[43]

---

39. This last question is posed in Azzouni, "Thick Epistemic Access."
40. White, "Locus," 293.
41. Hartshorne, *Creative Synthesis*, xix.
42. White, "Locus," 291.
43. This paper was initially prepared for a seminar on Heidegger at the Institute for Christian Studies, Toronto.

5

A comparison between Euclid and Aquinas and a question of method

THERE IS SOMETHING ABOUT mathematics' relation to our minds, to the universe and perhaps even to God that allows the study of its history to impact us in far-reaching ways. Developments in mathematics (such as non-Euclidean geometry and chaos patterns in fractals) have managed to change the very ways in which humans conceive the universe. Since mathematics does not develop in a vacuum, the history of mathematics also has the potential to illuminate virtually every discipline, not least philosophy and theology. Twentieth-century Roman Catholic theologian Bernard Lonergan, for example, is representative of a long line of thinkers who have understood the significance of mathematics and its history for philosophy and theology. His own conviction is that "the transition from common sense and theory to interiority promotes us from consciousness of self to knowledge of self."[1] Yet Lonergan urges that "[i]t is not enough to have acquired common sense and to speak ordinary language":

> One has also to examine mathematics, and discover what is happening when one is learning it and, again, what was happening as it was being developed. From reflecting on mathematics one has to go on to reflecting on natural science, discern its procedures . . . From the precision of mathematical understanding and thought and from the ongoing, cumulative advance of natural science, one has to turn to the procedures of common sense, grasp how it differs from mathematics and natural science, discern its proper

---

1. Lonergan, *Method*, 259.

A comparison between Euclid and Aquinas and a question of method

procedures, the range of its relevance, the permanent risk it runs of merging with nonsense.[2]

I understand Lonergan to be saying here that mathematics and its history can serve as a very useful foil for a number of disciplinary endeavors. Comparisons between mathematics and other disciplines can not only enrich one's understanding of a particular disciplinary endeavor, but it may also reveal a thing or two about the person undertaking the endeavor. In an effort to show just how perceptive Lonergan is here, I set out below to illustrate how the history of mathematics can prove instructive for philosophers and theologians, by suggesting 1) that behind the metaphors of proof and certainty lurks a substantial subjective element in mathematics (and if this is the case in mathematics, how much more is this the case in philosophy and theology!), and 2) certain results in mathematics can offer food for thought for philosophy and theology with respect to how these ought *not* to be done. The following involves a constructive comparison between Euclid's *Elements* and Aquinas' *Summa*.

All throughout the history of Western philosophy, those philosophers who were conversant with the mathematics of their time could not help but be impressed with the way that mathematics proceeds, time and again, to produce results that have a different sense of validity and necessity about them that results of any other discipline do not.[3] Even today, mathematics is popularly depicted as a field of inquiry that establishes its tenets *necessarily*. Compare how people like to use the phrase, "mathematical certainty," referring to the utter reliability associated with proven mathematical results. Historically speaking, Euclid's *Elements* is considered the earliest example for this type of investigation.

On another front, Aquinas' *Summa Contra Gentiles* (hereafter *SCG*) is a good example of how dialectical investigations have been carried out in philosophy and theology. Yet, curiously enough, the works of Euclid and Aquinas are rarely considered together. What is Aquinas doing in *SCG*? Could it be that Aquinas was actually trying, insofar as his material would allow him, to mimic the structure of Euclid's *Elements*, a geometric compendium for which his teacher, Albert Magnus, had written a commentary?

---

2. Longeran, *Method*, 260.

3. A great example of this (taken from the seventeenth-century) is Spinoza's *Tractatus Theologico-Politicus*.

Blaise Pascal, centuries later, was of the opinion that

> ... geometry alone knows the true rules of reasoning, and, without limiting itself to the rules of syllogism ... limits itself and bases itself on the true method of conducting reasonings in all things ... and which is so advantageous to know that we find by experience that between minds of equal strength, when all things are equal, the one which possesses geometry surpasses the other, and acquires a completely new strength.[4]

Pythagoras, Plato, Aristotle and Proclus believed something like this; did Aquinas believe it too? Perhaps a cursory comparison of the *Elements* and *SCG* can shed some light on what Aquinas appears to be doing in *SCG* and what medieval philosophers may have thought generally with respect to what it was that they were doing when they did what we might call today philosophical theology.

In Euclid's *Elements*, there are two types of proofs: a proof of demonstration (QED) and a proof of construction (QEF). The former aims to show that a given proposition is true, and the latter that a thing proposed can be constructed. One way to help English readers distinguish which of the two is involved for a given proposition is to note whether the proposition contains a finite verb. For example, Proposition 5 of Book 3 reads: "If two circles cut one another, they will not have the same centre." The finite verb in the English translation, "will not have," is the clue that we are in for a QED. By contrast, Proposition 1 of the same book simply reads: "To find a centre of a given circle." This proposition does not have a finite verb but begins with the infinitive "to find." Likewise, the first proposition of the first book reads: "On a given finite straight line to construct an equilateral triangle." Such propositions are proven by construction.

The "showing" involved in a constructive proof is of a different sort than that provided by demonstration. Although they both have demonstrative force, the way in which a construction elicits assent is palpably different from the way a demonstration does. It is a showing by *doing* and not so much by reasoning. The burden of such proofs is to show that *to do* a thing is *possible* and that license can be granted to do it as needed. Geometers resort to demonstration when they want to show that a geometrical object *necessarily* has some particular property so long as this or that condition obtains.

---

4. Pascal, *Pascal Selections*, 174.

A comparison between Euclid and Aquinas and a question of method

It has been said that Thomas Hobbes once opened a copy of Book 1 of the *Elements* to the part that treats the Pythagorean Theorem and was amazed that such a thing could be true. After intently studying the theorem, he worked his way *backwards* through the book from that proposition (which is toward the end of the first book) until he finally reached the first proposition (which is toward the beginning of the first book) and, by doing this, became satisfied that the theorem was true. This is a common pedagogical strategy used today in high school geometry; I propose to do something similar with a cluster of propositions from *SCG* to help readers better understand what it is that Aquinas is doing in this work and how it differs from a geometric presentation. To do this, let us begin with chapter 45 of book 2, which concludes the true first cause of the distinction of things, and work our way back to chapter 40, which explains that matter cannot be the first cause of the distinction of things.

Let us compare Aquinas' claim here—"The true first cause of the distinction of things"—with the other five under consideration (chapters 44–40, proceeding backwards). The others have an implicit verb-like structure provided by the opening conjunctive "that": "That the distinction of things does not . . ."; "That the distinction of things is not . . ."; "That the first cause . . . is not . . ."; and so on. These seem the syntactical equivalents to Euclidean proofs of demonstration and play analogously the same role in Aquinas as proofs of demonstration do in Euclid. However, when one reads through the rest of chapter 45, it does not strike one as any such proof at all.

"No creature can be equal to God," says Aquinas. "[T]hat which is in the cause, simply and unitedly, exists in the effect in composite and multiple fashion—unless the effect attain to the species of the cause." In other words, God, as the "most perfect agent," had to create in multiplicity in order for his magnificent perfection to shine through his creation. The "perfect likeness of God" can only be actualized in the universe by way of multiple things; and this is precisely what Scripture teaches, according to Aquinas, in Gen 1. "Then, too," argues Aquinas, "a thing approaches to God's likeness the more perfectly as it resembles Him in more things." Since God is the highest good, the things that are in the universe are similarly more good because there are other things amongst or toward which they can contribute to the good. In other words, if some thing is not only good in itself, but also helps another thing tend toward its good, it would clearly be more good than if it were only good in itself. Several more such arguments are adduced and these are confirmed by Gen 1:31.

Yet as I understand Aristotle, he would most certainly say that Aquinas' interpretation (i.e., the traditional Christian interpretation) of Gen 1 is *not* fitting for God. Rather, the primary body is that which is furthest from the earth and is ungenerated. For Aristotle, again as I understand him, the "perfect likeness of God" is the ungeneratedness and indestructibility of perfection that any deity would co-possess with the outermost heavens. The problem would be—and it is a real problem—how could Aquinas' God create something totally new, something so unlike himself? Chances are that Aristotle would not have agreed to an interpretation of the universe along the lines proposed by Gen 1. For starters, the thing caused is so fundamentally and utterly different from the cause itself. This is, to say the least, a very non-Aristotelian construal.

Yet Aquinas' argument is that God *is* the cause of the distinction in things and he is of the opinion that it *is* fitting that things should be this way. Aquinas surmises: "The diversity and equality in created things are not the result of chance, nor of a diversity of matter, nor of the intervention of certain causes or merits, but of the intention of God Himself, who wills to give the creature such perfection as it is possible for it to have." "From the foregoing it can be shown what is truly the first cause of the distinction of things," writes Aquinas. But this comes across as a process of elimination argument; it is not a proof of demonstration. So what kind of proof is it, if it is a proof at all?

Aquinas claims that *it can be shown* that God is truly the first cause of the distinction of things. Given my interest in the way the history of math impinges upon the history of philosophy, I want to ask, is this some kind of proof of construction or perhaps something different altogether? Is Aquinas trying to "show" by *doing*? I say he is. He urges that *it is fitting* that God is truly the first cause of the distinction of things. Is this anything more than a logical possibility? If not, he may be in trouble, for possibility alone carries little to no argumentative force in philosophy. Yet in Aquinas' mind, all other candidates for the cause of the distinction of things have been discounted. So what role might logical possibility play in a theological proof of construction? I find this to be a very interesting question since precisely what Aquinas says *is* fitting for God, Aristotle says is *not* fitting for God. This is significant because whereas Anselm, for example, had the honor of feudal lords in mind when he referred to what would be fitting for God, Aquinas surely has Aristotle's first agent in mind and purports, among other things, that when Aristotle is correctly interpreted he is absolutely compatible with Christianity.

In the passage under investigation, Aquinas is setting up a cumulative process of elimination. Chapters 44–40 (working backwards) each seek to disqualify a causal contender from theoretical consideration. Chapter 45 proffers the alternative, the only cause remaining, a cause that Aquinas sees to be eminently fitting. Put another way, chapter 45 aims to show that God as first cause of distinction is eminently possible, and not only *possible*, but that, given the problems that the other answers face, a license may be granted to readers to believe it. Let us take a quick peek at these other answers and recall the problems Aquinas finds with them.

Is the accrual of merits the cause of the distinction in things? Here Aquinas counters Origen's claim that "God, of His goodness alone, first made all creatures equal . . . and these by their free choice were moved in various ways . . . and as a result of this, diverse grades in spiritual substances were established by the divine justice . . ." Aquinas reminds readers, however, that priority must always be given to the higher good. The greatest good is the perfection of the universe. That good, achieved by the diversity of things, occurs by way of the intentions of the first agent. Aquinas directs further arguments at Origen: if Origen were to have held his position truly, he would not be consistent with other beliefs he promulgates. According to Thomas, it would not be fitting for God to make an imperfect world, and he appeals to Gen for support.

Could secondary agents have introduced forms into matter? Aquinas argues that secondary agents could not have done this. In order for a secondary agent to cause distinctions, form and matter would both have to be available to it. Since being is the "first among effects" and all being requires forms, the first agent must have caused forms originally. Moreover, since being requires both forms and matter, some kind of diversity must have preexisted all secondary agents. Prime matter only exists potentially; without forms, it cannot be actualized. Aquinas also appeals to Gen and Col.

Perhaps, the plain fact that there even is a world of secondary agents is responsible for the diversity of the furniture of the universe. Aquinas confutes this position as well: Effects must be proportionate to their causes. The order of the universe is such that it is an effect that it is only worthy of the first agent. One is not free to claim that multiplicity is a shortcoming of the universe since order and diversity are the highest good. And even if diversities are caused by secondary agents, their causes are subject to the intentions of the causes of the first agent. Aquinas cites Gen and Job.

Could the distinction of things be explained by multiple agents acting in contrary ways? The contrariety of agents cannot account for the distinction in things either. Again, Aquinas invokes the orderedness of the universe. In Aquinas' mind, order argues against accidental causes. If it were to be the case that contrarieties caused the distinction in things, they must act together in contrary ways simultaneously. If they do not, then the contrary who acts first would be the first agent, which is what Aquinas is arguing in the first place. Otherwise, the second contrary would be the cause, but secondary agents have already been discounted since in chapter 15 it was shown that "God is to all things the cause of being." Aquinas stresses that diversity is a fitting expression of perfection and that there is no reason to invoke multiple causes, especially contrary ones, in an attempt to account for diversity. Aquinas invokes Isa, Eccl and Amos.

Matter cannot cause forms; matter can only cause matter. No diversity can result from matter alone. In the absence of an agent's intention, chance must be involved in the distinction of things, but this has already been ruled out in chapter 39 of book 2. The higher perfections and/or goods are served by the lower ones: matter, being the lowest, cannot prove an end in itself. When it does show itself thus, it does so only fortuitously. This is well known. Aquinas refers to no scripture here.

Thus, chapters 44–40 present the eliminative arms of Aquinas' argument by elimination. Perhaps they function as proofs of demonstration. They may not be axiomatic but they are deductive enough. However, in chapter 45, where one might most expect to see a proof of demonstration, we find instead an analogous construction. Aquinas notes in one of his commentaries on Aristotle that "in these sciences [viz. geometry] those things are postulated which are first in the genus of quantity . . . Once these are postulated, certain other things are sought through demonstration, such as the equilateral triangle and the square…In these cases the demonstrations are said to be, as it were, operational . . ."[5] But, in our chapter 45, Aquinas has to show *that* something is true and this typically

---

5. Aquinas, *Commentary to Posterior Anayltics*.

A comparison between Euclid and Aquinas and a question of method

requires a QED. Yet Aquinas seems to have no choice but to provide an *operational* QEF, a proof of construction, as it were, because it is the best that one can do in response to the problem at hand. It goes without saying that Aquinas is not actually constructing a figure to show that it is possible, but he is constructing this section of *SCG* to show that God as cause of diversity is *possible* and that given the alternatives, it becomes a plausible answer to the question at hand. No one has yet plausibly answered how there can be a diversity of things in the world, according to Aquinas: the answers that have been proffered simply cannot be accepted. The catholic Christian faith has an answer that is possible, but not *merely* possible—that is, *if* one is properly disposed to accept it, *if* one has been following the argumentative trajectory set by Aquinas' various arguments as part of an honest and open quest for the truth. To such, an operational license should be granted to believe that God is the true cause of the distinction in things.

When Hibbs reads *SCG*, he discerns a dialectically-driven narrative structure. He explains, "[*SCG*] addresses the fundamental question of antiquity and the Middle Ages. Among all of Thomas's works, only the *Summa contra Gentiles* focuses extensively on the great debate of antiquity over the best way of life and over who teaches authoritatively concerning the highest good." Hibbs calls this dialectic concern "wisdom"; Hadot considers it a "spiritual exercise"; while Levering describes it as a "wisdom-exercise."[6] How about a "spiritual proof of construction"? Geometry proceeds ideally by deduction, but proofs of construction are generically accepted on the *intuited* basis of a particular construction—a proof that runs from the particular construct that is devised at the time of proof to a generic construct that is accepted by the mind. Chapter 45 in Aquinas' *SCG* seems to me to proceed in an analogous way, and this comes as no surprise; for when one inquires into the argumentative tack taken by medieval Muslim contemporaries one finds a very similar thing.

According to Gyekye, the medieval Arabic philosopher, al-Farabi, observes that when working with syllogisms, a philosopher should not be as concerned with the truth of a conclusion as with its validity. Medieval theologians, however, were always preoccupied with the *truths* of their conclusions. In order to conform to philosophic expectations that an argument be formally valid, Muslim theologians, according to al-Farabi,

6. See Hibbs, "Kretzmann's Theism"; Hadot, *Philosophy*; and Matthew Levering, *Scripture*.

would arrange their arguments so that although they were dialectical in nature, they were presented syllogistically in form. Gyekye explains, "According to [both] Aristotle and al-Farabi, dialectical arguments, though syllogistically correct, fall short of the conditions of scientific accuracy; hence al-Farabi's pleas for 'tolerance,' that is, a less rigid approach in search of inaccuracy or truth." In spite of this, al-Farabi observes that philosophical theologians have the inclination to be more ambitious in their claims than philosophers insofar as they desire to get more out of their dialectical engagements than merely an argument to the effect that their interlocutor's premise is false.

Aquinas undoubtedly faces similar tensions. SCG superficially reads as if it is a long, deductive train of theological propositions, yet it lacks the demonstrative force associated with such propositions, at least, when such are presented in geometry. That is because the form is operational only, I say. This is to be expected and is not unlike how his contemporaries proceeded. According to Gyekye, the medieval Muslim philosopher-theologians were torn by their convictions to the effect that they believed in the "logically perfect nature of apodeictic method on the one hand, and the logically imperfect (defective) nature of analogical reasoning on the other." This "led them to utilize the resources of the former by casting their [analogical] arguments in syllogistic molds."[7] Although medieval philosophers would have liked to avail themselves of the demonstrative punch typified by Aristotle in his discussions of mathematics, dialectical responses were the best they could ever muster.

But this is not necessarily a bad place to be. Many disciplines have this same ideal in mind (and this is, of course, all very Aristotelian): to be able to state explicitly its first principles and to show how the entire discipline follows deductively from them. For example, Albert Einstein explained before the Physical Society in Berlin that "[t]he supreme task of the physicist is to arrive at those universal elementary laws from which the cosmos can be built up by pure deduction." The problem, he explains, is that "[t]here is no logical path to these laws; only intuition, resting on sympathetic understanding of experience, can reach them."[8] Yet there is a huge difference with regard to what degree each of the disciplines can manage this state of affairs. The history of science shows that although

7. Gyekye, "Al-Farabi," 43.
8. Cited in Northrop, "Einstein's Conception," 401.

there may be several scientific theories competing for acceptance at any given time, eventually only one is able to gain the ascendency. The history of math, for its part, shows that mathematics has an intrinsic flexibility about it that can sometimes allow multiple theories to coexist, sometimes indefinitely, without a decision so long as the theories are consistent, can be proven, and are serviceable for science (or some other application).[9]

Unfortunately, philosophy and theology are not so lucky. In these two disciplines, disputed questions are hardly ever met with consensus and are hardly ever *proven* in one direction or another, so much so that thinkers like Kant can begin wondering whether metaphysics as a disciplinary endeavor is even possible. And so we are brought to the precipice of the Thomistic existential crisis, as it were, the one that Lonergan talks about so well: "[W]hile dialectic does reveal the polymorphism of human consciousness—the deep and unreconcilable oppositions on religious, moral, and intellectual issues—still it does no more: it does not take sides. It is *the person* [italics mine] that takes sides . . ."[10] How one decides depends on one's foundational *conversion*, says Lonergan, and this is the case everywhere, I say—even in math in certain cases (that is, if people can be candid enough about it). It is just that the predicament is so much more conspicuous in philosophy and theology. That is why someone like Montaigne would complain: "It is very easy, upon accepted foundations, to build what you please . . . For our masters occupy and win beforehand as much room in our belief as they need in order to conclude afterward whatever they wish, in the manner of the geometricians with their axioms."[11]

For a modern day example, consider Christopher Small of the department of Statistics at the University of Waterloo, who admits: "There is a certain sense in which no proof can ever be deemed valid if its conclusions are sufficiently unpalatable . . . On the other hand, those who find the conclusions of an argument particularly appealing have often been accepting of its premises"—and those who find the conclusions troubling do not.[12] Salmon imagines how this might be done:

---

9. See, for example, Dieks, "Flexibility."
10. Lonergan, *Method*, 268.
11. de Montaigne, *Complete Works*, 403.
12. See Small, "Reflections."

> For that matter, even if there is an effective test [for determining whether a proof is really a proof], its mere existence does not put an end to the infinite regress of demanding a proof, then demanding a proof that the first proof is correct, then demanding a proof that the second proof is correct, and so on. Nor does the existence of an effective test for proofs eliminate the possibility of justified doubt in a given case. To quell such doubt the test has to be applied to the proof in question. One may then question whether the test has been applied correctly. And even if one is satisfied that it was, one may justifiably doubt whether the purported test itself is correct.[13]

This suggests that behind the metaphors of proof and certainty, there is a subjective judgment to be made with regard to whether the implications of a proof are acceptable. Christopher Small observes that if this is how things go in the field of mathematics, how much more does it happen in philosophy and theology?

Lonergan highlights the inexorable facet of personal involvement in dialectic: ". . . the side [a person] takes will depend on the fact that he has or has not been converted . . . [Conversion] is a decision about whom and what you are for and, again, whom and what you are against. It is a decision illuminated by the manifold possibilities exhibited in dialectic."[14] Perhaps that is why it is said that "every idle word that men shall speak, they shall give account thereof in the day of judgment" (Matt 12:36), which means to say (as Lonergan puts it), "Arbitrariness is just unauthenticity."[15] This is something that conversion should effectively preclude.

To sum up, a comparison of the *Elements* and the *Summa Contra Gentiles* can help show how much philosophy and theology differ from mathematics in the extent to which one will be able to offer proof for a conclusion; how easily one will be able to convincingly argue others for a particular set of controlling assumptions; and how the dialectical decisions philosophers and theologians make tend to reveal something of the participants' existential predisposition.[16]

---

13. Salmon, *Metaphysics*, 263.
14. Lonergan, *Method*, 268.
15. Ibid.
16. A version of this paper was presented at a regional meeting of the American Academy of Religion held at McGill University, May 2005, and later incorporated into a published article, "Two Examples of How the History of Mathematics Can Inform Theology," *Theology and Science* 8 (2010): 69–84. Used by permission.

6

On the "good and necessary consequence" clause in the Westminster Confession of Faith (1647)

THERE IS A FLIER for a conference that I came across describing the intellectual milieu of the seventeenth century in these words: "Skeptical questions about the natural world were often stated in terms of whether one can deduce from one's representations alone that there exists a natural world outside ourselves that causes us to have these representations in the first place."[1] In 1637 Rene Descartes ponders:

> Those long chains of reasons, all simple and easy, which geometers have habitually used to reach the most difficult proofs gave me occasion to imagine to myself that everything which could fall under human knowledge would follow in the same way and that, provided only that one refused to accept anything as true which was not and that one always kept to the order necessary to deduce one thing from another, there would not be anything so far distant that one could not finally reach it, not so hidden that one could not discover it.[2]

By 1687, Isaac Newton is writing: "But hitherto I have not been able to discover the cause of those properties of gravity from phenomena, and I frame no hypotheses; *for whatever is not deduced from the phenomena,* is to be called an hypothesis; and hypotheses, whether metaphysical or physical, whether of occult qualities or mechanical, have no place in experimental philosophy."[3] Leibniz, too, in 1675, urges in a letter that to

---

1. *Filosofiska Institutionen.*
2. Descartes, *Discourse on Method*, Part 2.
3. Newton, *Principia*, 428.

successfully engage in philosophical meditations "it is good to proceed in order and to establish propositions; that is the way to gain ground and to make sure progress."[4]

And let us not forget about Pascal who in 1657 writes:

> The method for not erring is sought by everyone. The logicians claim to lead to it, the geometers alone to reach it, and except for their science, and those that imitate it, there are no genuine demonstrations. And the entire art is the precepts alone that we have stated: they alone suffice, they alone prove; all other rules are useless or harmful. That is what I know from a long experience of all sorts of books and persons.[5]

Into this cultural matrix enters the Westminster Confession of Faith (1647): "The whole counsel of God concerning all things necessary for his own glory, man's salvation, faith and life, is either expressly set down in Scripture, or by good and necessary consequence may be deduced from Scripture: unto which nothing at any time is to be added, whether by new revelations of the Spirit, or traditions of men."[6] It would appear that the Westminster divines, as they are called, have thought it prudent to incorporate into a public confession the insistence that one is to look to scripture to find a set of axioms that are given by God, that have been "expressly set down" by him, and that from these axioms one can deduce the whole counsel of God.

Several Reformed writers try their best to downplay the novelty of approaching theology this way. For example, Richard Muller writes, "[T]he assumption . . . that the text of scripture provided principial or axiomatic truths from which right conclusions could be drawn for the sake of the formulation of Christian teaching . . . [can also be] found in both late Medieval and Reformation-era theology."[7] In *By Good and Necessary Consequence: A Preliminary Genealogy of Biblicist Foundationalism*, I cite these excerpts to bolster my suggestion that this is a theological innovation, made possible by specific social developments that transpire during the course of the late Renaissance. These would include intense cultural pressures for every discipline to conform, insofar as possible, to the likeness of mathematics.

---

4. Leibniz, *Philosophical Essays*, 5.
5. Pascal, *Selections*, 193.
6. *Westminster Confession of Faith*, 1.6
7. Muller, "Inspired by God," 58. I have inverted this sentence for readability.

On the "good and necessary consequence" clause

For present purposes, let us talk briefly about how, even if it were possible that theology should be made to look like mathematics (medieval theologians, such as Thomas Aquinas and his Arabic contemporaries, had already realized you cannot get away with this kind of thing in theology) it does not seem wise to expect "the whole counsel of God" to be something that theologians can deduce from a set of divinely given axioms expressly set forth in the Bible. Let us look to developments in mathematics to help see why.

Kurt Gödel claims the following:

> It is [the second incompleteness theorem] which makes the incompletability of mathematics particularly evident. For, it makes it impossible that someone should set up a certain well-defined system of axioms and rules and consistently make the following assertion about it: All of these axioms and rules I perceive (with mathematical certitude) to be correct, and moreover I believe that they contain all of mathematics.[8]

According to Salmon, there are certain mathematical truths that are known to be correct with mathematical certainty that are not dependent upon the correctness of any other mathematical propositions; these are intuited as such by our mathematical capacities and known to be true solely through them. From these and only these, all other humanly knowable mathematical propositions can strictly be deduced using accepted mathematical rules of reasoning. But if these axiomatic truths can be expressed in such a way so that they are recursive and consistent, then the mathematical proposition that states that these axioms are correct (which is not itself among the axioms) can never be deduced from those axioms. That proposition would either need to be added on as a new axiom or proven by another meta-theory. Thus no formal system can contain all of mathematics.

I surmise that a rather strong parallel suggests itself between this mathematical development and the situation that transpires in the kind of Reformed theology that the Westminster Confession requires of its adherents (as part of a confession!), especially if the "whole counsel of God" can be expressed as a formal system with the expressly set down truths found in scripture invoked as the axioms. Whatever set of rules of theological reasoning lie behind the good and necessary consequence

---

8. Cited in Salmon, *Metaphysics*, 246.

deduction mentioned by the Westminster Confession would presumably be ones that the Westminster divines could agree upon (else they would have never been submitted for inclusion in a confession). How to show that the axioms can be satisfactorily, formally enumerated and that they are recursive, of course, remains to be seen.

That said, philosophers and theologians should give more attention to Standberg and others (scientists and mathematicians) when they chime in, saying that religion and science do not *really* converge, whether with respect to Einstein's relativity, to Heisenberg's uncertainty, or to Gödel's incompleteness.[9] Even so, there may still be some useful *parallels* to take note of. Franzen, Raatikainen, and others are continually reminding us that Gödel's theorems *only apply to systems that involve higher arithmetical statements.*[10] Taking some time to reflect upon the matter, we should agree that it does not take Gödel's theorem to *suggest* (not *prove*!) that the whole counsel of God cannot be deduced from an enumerable set of axioms allegedly given expressly by scripture. Even so, comparing this with Gödel's theorem does not seem to me a meaningless endeavor. Some logicians who write on Gödel's theorem love to say that it is *trivially* true that the Bible is not complete, but that is not always an easy thing to hear, especially for someone who belongs to a community that adheres to the Westminster Confession, for example. (In fact, they might even dispute it.) Gödel's theorem is not needed to show that scripture is incomplete, the logicians say. Yet just as some philosophers and theologians may have misjudged the scope of Gödel's theorem in their applications of it to various disciplines, perhaps the logicians, too, misunderstand philosophy and theology and how philosophers and theologians are not typically interested in proofs. They are after analogical and dialectical arguments. Not only that, but some may not realize that, at least since Plato, there have always been philosophers who consciously look to mathematics and science in an attempt to help keep their philosophy and theology from "merging into nonsense," as Lonergan puts it.

There are numerous models for doing philosophy. As Harry Redner explains, "Scientific models for philosophy have been as influential as literary ones right from the beginning."[11] Philosophers and theolo-

---

9. Strandberg, "Religion and Science."
10. Franzén, *Gödel's Theorem*; Raatikainen, "Philosophical Relevance."
11. Redner, *Ends of Philosophy*, 327.

gians should be encouraged to look to mathematics and its history for creative ideas on how to do and how *not* to do philosophy and theology. The mathematicians who complain that philosophy and theology cannot use Gödel's theorems because these only apply to higher arithmetic systems are not only misidentifying philosophic method with mathematical method but also confusing philosophy with method. Redner observes that sometimes "[p]hilosophies may be so dominated by their model that they are in danger of completely identifying themselves with it and this leads to assertions that philosophy is really geometry, or logic, or methodology."[12] But he urges that this is not an attitude to emulate! When mathematicians complain that philosophy is not number theory and that Gödel's theorems do not prove anything in philosophy and theology, well that seems to me like a refreshing thing to admit! Philosophy is not number theory (just as it is not literature). Yet that does not imply that Gödel's theorems do not have *anything* to say to philosophers and theologians.

Even so, in a discussion like the present one there is no reason to simply leave it at that. For number theory is not the only field that has an incompleteness theorem. Computer science has one also. (And there happens to be an ongoing feud of sorts between the two fields over what implications can be drawn from incompleteness.) Computer scientists are not as reluctant to go from their version of incompleteness to domains of human activity that go *beyond* number theory. Gregory Chaitin, for example, judges that one conclusion that can be drawn from Gödel's theorems is that "Hilbert was wrong and Poincaré was right: intuition cannot be eliminated from mathematics, *or from human thought in general* [italics mine]."[13] So Chaitin thinks that implications from incompleteness can apply equally well to activities outside mathematics; in his view, incompleteness is such a fundamental feature of *information* that it can be said to describe "human thought in general." Ruelle explains:

> What Chaitin showed is that assertions of the type "The message 'blah blah blah . . .' has a [Kolmogorov-Chaitin] complexity of at least N" are either false, or unprovable when N is sufficiently large. How large is sufficiently large? That depends on the axioms of your theory. Your axioms contain a certain amount of information (depending on their total length), and you cannot prove that 'blah

---

12. Redner, *Ends of Philosophy*, 327, 328.
13. Chaitin, *Meta Math!* 146.

blah blah . . .' contains more information than the axioms you are using.[14]

I understand this to mean that when a person is going to begin talking about his or her formal theory in a meta-theoretical way, then that person will either have to begin saying things that are untrue or things that are unprovable—at least from within that formal theory. And this uncanny property is not restricted to arithmetical systems. Rucker, a computer scientist, explains: given a handful of reasonable assumptions, "we can apply our undecidability corollary to *any* complex natural process!"[15] Stephen Wolfram, yet another computer scientist, claims: "[Gödel] left us the legacy of undecidability, which we now realize affects not just esoteric issues about mathematics, but also all sorts of questions in science, engineering, medicine and more."[16] Compare Wolfram's insight with Rucker's Principle of Natural Undecidability: "For most naturally occurring complex processes, and any consistent correct formal system for science, there will be sentences about the process that are undecidable by the given formal system."[17] Yet those who say that incompleteness extends beyond arithmetic are not all computer scientists; Gödel himself thought it appropriate to apply his theorems to the operations of the human mind. Nathan Salmon is a contemporary logician (a student of Alonzo Church and Saul Kripke) who thinks that Gödel was right in doing so.[18]

In any event, the analogy I am trying to draw between the Westminster Confession and Gödel's incompleteness boils down to this: when someone is told that they have to confess that "The whole counsel of God concerning all things necessary for his own glory, man's salvation, faith and life, is either expressly set down in Scripture, or by good and necessary consequence may be deduced from Scripture," it appears that that person is being advised to confess something *about* scripture from within a theory that is (allegedly) expressly delineated by scripture. That suggests to me that the proposition asserted in the Westminster Confession is likely either false or not decidable (based on the axioms or the deduced propositions found within scripture). In other words, the proposition

---

14. Ruelle, *Chance and Chaos*, 147.
15. Rucker, *Lifebox*, 450.
16. Wolfram, "Gödel's 100th Birthday."
17. Rucker, *Lifebox*, 451.
18. For a defense of Gödel, see Salmon, *Metaphysics*, 243–268.

that one is being asked to confess in the Westminster Confession must be added as an additional axiom—to those propositions that are said to be expressly set down in scripture, except this one will not be set down in scripture, either expressly or inferentially. I am looking at Gödel's statement above and paraphrasing it to the following effect: "*It is not wise* that someone should look at evident precepts in the Bible (as if they were evident) and all that they entail and then turn and say: All of these precepts and rules of theological deduction I perceive to be correct, and moreover I believe that they contain the whole counsel of God." Such a claim, in all likelihood, presumes too much with respect to the nature and authority of scripture.

Not only that but persons from other faith communities have every right to question whether the claiming of that confessional proposition as a new axiom requires "proof" or whether the inclusion of the extra-biblical axiom belongs to the counsel of God. They might also inquire into how many other propositions from the counsel of God are not expressed in scripture, or what aspects of the counsel of God *are* to be found in scripture, and so on. These types of concerns have been raised by Catholics and Protestants over the centuries and even among Protestants themselves (but not always in the most amicable spirit). Yet when one pauses to consider the pattern of incompleteness found in mathematics and the various attempts to extend its implications to other domains of knowledge, it would seem that a critical reappraisal of theological deductivism such as the one prescribed in the Westminster Confession is in order. For a proposition that states that the whole counsel of God is set down in scripture is a proposition *about* axioms and as such may very well be a meaningless proposition—at least when asserted *from within the system that proposes those axioms to begin with*.[19] This suggests that the Westminster Confession plays the methodological role of a second formal system that tries to address axiomatic issues that scripture alone does not address. Whether one accepts or rejects this new meta-formal theory (the Westminster Confession) is a dialectical matter, and how one chooses among the available dialectical options at this level of theological discourse will be a function, as Lonergan would say, of one's *conversion*, which, to the say the least, is a complicated matrix of historical and cultural factors.

---

19. Compare Brisson and Meyerstein, *Inventing*, 179–180.

Ideas at the Intersection of Mathmatics, Philosophy, and Theology

So if someone asks, "How can the history of mathematics shed light on philosophy and theology?" the main thing I would like to note here is that there is a deductivist ideal for mathematics that is not appropriate for philosophy and theology. As Lonergan explains: "We can conceive philosophy that way, we can conceive theology that way, we can conceive mathematics that way, or physics, or any other science: the deductivist ideal. The question is, What is the value of it?"[20] The moral of the story for Lonergan is that "the history of mathematics and of science has been a matter of discovering that not everything is understood; not everything is an object of intelligence, something to understand," which leads him to *Insight*.[21] For us, though, our attention is drawn to a palpable tension between two different ways of conceiving and doing philosophy and theology. The deductive model is one way to proceed, a way that has been adapted from mathematics.[22] A dialectical model is another, and it belongs to philosophy proper. When philosophy and theology are carried out dialectically but with a metaphor of deductivism still in mind, acute tensions arise.

For example, philosophers and theologians typically proffer an ordered set of philosophical and theological propositions, but "Where do the proofs . . . come from?"[23] The metaphors of proof and certainty can entice some philosophers and theologians to attach to their conclusions an undue certainty. When this happens, theology betrays its mathematical model as metaphor. For confusion seems to arise between the certainty with which practitioners hold their various positions and the metaphorical nature of the mathematical models that are adapted for theology from mathematics. Philosophers and theologians carry out their work dialectically and analogically, yet the mathematician lays down objective rules for everyone to follow so that they can work together and get the same results.[24] As we have seen the latter approach is what some Protestant confessions have tried to accomplish for Protestantism, but

20. Lonergan, *Phenomenology*, 56.
21. Lonergan, *Phenomenology*, 61.
22. Brown considers "models" as extended metaphors. See Brown, *Making Truth*.
23. Lonergan continues: "One argument comes from working up one way, and another one from working up another way; one has one set of premises, and another one has another set of premises. The arguments are deductive arguments but they come from all over the map." See Lonergan, *Phenomenology*, 121.
24. Lonergan, *Phenomenology*, 20.

history shows that they have met with anything but optimal results. It was inevitable that practitioners would arrive at a multiplicity of results.[25] For there is considerably more wiggle room in philosophy and theology than there is in mathematics. Not only that, but if the amount of wiggle room available to mathematicians is more than the adapted metaphors of proof and certainty allow (for making subjective judgments regarding proofs' acceptability and whether the axioms are well-suited), then the wiggle room available to philosophers and theologians probably remains underappreciated, crying out for further examination.

One last consideration bears mentioning, one that Lonergan also discusses in his writings: if you offer people a philosophy or theology that ties people down and constrains what they are trying to do in their respective disciplines, "they will pull away from you and do as they please; they will be in revolt." But if you offer a philosophy or theology that does not quench the spirit of inquiry, "then you are doing your job."[26]

Leibniz observed there is a downside to modeling philosophy and theology after a deductive, mathematical ideal, weaknesses he thought that were evident in Descartes' work, for example: "As for myself, I cherished mathematics only because I found in it the traces of *the art of invention in general*; and it seems to me that I discovered, in the end, that Descartes himself had not yet penetrated the mystery of this great science."[27] In fact, "There have been many beautiful discoveries since Descartes, but, as far as I know, not one of them has come from a true Cartesian."[28] There is much to learn here, for theologians especially. For one might reasonably suppose that there are many beautiful theological discoveries to be made. What a shame it would truly be if not one of them were to come from a true theologian![29]

---

25. Compare Abraham, *Canon*.
26. Lonergan, *Phenomenology*, 127.
27. Leibniz, *Philosophical Essays*, 236.
28. Leibniz, *Philosophical Essays*, 240.
29. This paper was initially prepared for an invited lecture at the Franciscan University of Steubenville in November, 2008, and subsequently incorporated into a published article, "Two Examples of How the History of Mathematics Can Inform Theology," *Theology and Science* 8 (2010): 69–84. Used by permission.

7

Thoughts on supernaturalism and its irrelevance for science and mathematics

RELIGIOUS PEOPLE TEND TO be suspicious of science and mathematics, partly because the two disciplines have few places where a person's faith can play an active role. One reason for this is that religious beliefs posit the existence of supernatural beings and the existence of a supreme being, God. These beliefs persuade believers to adopt theological supernaturalism (TS), that is, the understanding and expectation that God can and does act in the world in ways that are not in accordance with those events that people typically witness during the course of their lifetimes.

These divine actions, it should be noted, may not always entail the "breaking" of natural laws. In fact, the more sophisticated interpretations of divine providence tend to steer clear of the notion of "natural" (whose opposite would be "supernatural") and suggest as alternatives "regular" and "irregular" or "usual" and "unusual" events.[1] Even so, divine actions are popularly believed to be the result of God acting outside nature, outside the universe—transcendent in some way—intentionally causing or influencing events that occur in nature, within the universe, according to his sovereign intentions. In spite of the fact that there are numerous theories of divine providence and divine action (and that most of them tend to be speculative), in popular culture at least, most believers would interpret divine agency through more of a supernatural framework than a naturalistic one.[2]

To take one example, Jim Burns, a popular Christian writer and radio host in the US, answers a college student's question about miracles

---
1. See, for example, Happel, "Divine Providence."
2. See Clayton, "Natural Law."

as follows: "I'm not an authority in theology, so I would suggest you talk with your pastor. But I can give your question my best shot. I believe the world you and I live in is much *more* than it appears. The Bible speaks of two worlds, the physical one that we live in and an unseen spiritual realm."[3] This is *the* signature religious belief, which leads believers to infer the position of TS. "[T]he world you and I live in is much *more* than it appears" ; therefore, there is plenty of room for the miraculous.

TS can convey different things to different people, but for the purposes of this paper let it signify the following ubiquitous belief: there are two realms, one physical and one spiritual, and the spiritual domain that is somehow above and beyond the world of everyday experience is the "place" where God resides. A problem that religious people have with science and mathematics, then, is that these two disciplines do not have any interest in events that require the spiritual realm to exist in any real way that matters. In other words, they exclude God from everything that they study.

On a very basic level, science and mathematics will always be in potential conflict with religion. Historically, the relation of science and mathematics to religion may have been ambiguous,[4] but the *pathos* in the West toward the relation between science and religion seems to have become antagonistic. Religionists of almost every persuasion all struggle with how to reconcile their religious understandings of the world with scientific explanations of causes and mathematical descriptions of forces that are claimed to be operative in the same world where God is said to be providentially acting.

Accordingly, a number of religious thinkers have set their sights on methodological naturalism (MN) as TS's chief philosophical nemesis.[5] This is precisely because methodological naturalism involves, among other things, a social contract among scientists to disallow TS methodologically in all activities involving science and mathematics. In other words, *qua* scientist and mathematician, an investigator is asked to suspend all beliefs (if she has them) that pertain to the spiritual realm and with respect to whether spiritual beings exist while doing science and

---

3. Burns, "Aren't Miracles," 22.

4. See Bozeman, *Protestants*; Boiler, *American Thought*; Brooke, *Science and Religion*; Young, *Biblical Flood*.

5. See, for example, Moreland, "Theistic Science"; Plantinga, "Methodological Naturalism?"; Clayton, *God*, 171–186; and Griffin, *Religion*.

mathematics. Practitioners are to proceed methodologically in empirical or mathematical research with the express understanding that "natural" causes and relations are the only ones permitted for the description of any phenomenon that might be observed or for any theoretical description of physical events that might be derived. MN has been widely accepted among scientists and mathematicians precisely because it is not clear how TS would make any difference to the work that is being done. In other words, it is not clear whether meaningful contributions to scientific or mathematical findings would be made if appeals to TS replaced MN.

Other religious writers see things differently. They are not persuaded that MN poses a real threat to TS since the activities with which science regularly engages are not "purely" scientific anyway. Scientists and mathematicians almost always intersect with other areas of inquiry as they carry out their work, such as ethics, politics, philosophy and theology, to name a few. Other writers do not believe that MN can exclude TS since there is a conceptual vagueness that plagues terms commonly used in scientific discourse, such as "explanation" and "cause." Still other writers argue that because science is based upon a specific set of metaphysical assumptions, it cannot coherently promote MN. Otherwise, MN will be in direct conflict with the underlying metaphysical principles that legitimate science in the first place. The most common strategy, however, on the part of religious writers is to argue for the impossibility of demarcating science as a discipline from other "non-scientific" fields. Yet in spite of these more conciliatory approaches, MN still appears to be the source of religious persons' distrust of science and mathematics.

Be that as it may, no one seems to be claiming that MN is *completely* wrong. Philip Clayton observes, for example, that "[t]he question . . . is not whether there is any presumption of naturalism but how strong we should make it and in what areas we should regard it to be strongest."[6] One thing is sure. More and more are developing a "fear and loathing of God-of-the-gaps theology."[7] They tend to reason as follows: "Only the assumption that there must be some natural explanation can motivate the sort of scientific research that eventually led to the discovery of the DNA structure."[8] Not

6. Clayton, *God*, 172.
7. Plantinga, "Methodological Naturalism?"
8. Clayton, *God*, 174. Compare Palevitz, "Science Versus Religion." For defenses of God-of-the-gaps arguments, see Reynolds, "God of the Gaps," and Moreland, "Complementarity."

only that, but God-of-the-gaps theology is often portrayed as a last ditch effort for religious persons to stave off unpalatable implications drawn from science and mathematics arrived at through MN.

It is important to bear in mind that God-of-the-gaps theology is not the belief that God *only* acts in those places where scientists and mathematicians are at a loss for explanation. That kind of God-of-the-gaps approach might be more fruitfully called "God-*most-obviously*-in-the-gaps." From a naïve, religious perspective at least, it might seem that God is more "obviously" at work in the gaps. Yet it would be more theologically correct to say that God is fundamentally at work *all the time*, even where there are no gaps in our knowledge.

Is it helpful for believers to take a "God-most-obviously-in-the-gaps" approach to science and mathematics? This is hard to say. Even the most pious believer will admit that there is an ever-present danger of religious concerns stopping science in its tracks. It does not seem reasonable to expect scientists and mathematicians to appeal to supernaturalism every time they are at a "serious" loss for explanation. Mathematician-philosopher William Dembski proposed something like this. He suggested that scientists could run their ideas through an explanatory filter and, depending on how it fared, actually stop looking for "natural" explanations.[9] A God-of-the-gaps science of this kind would be a science that accepts *super*natural "explanations" as a scientifically meaningful part of its discourse. It may be very comforting for religious people to think that there will always be evidence for God in the areas of inquiry where answers are lacking, but at the same time, it provides us insight into why religious believers distrust science and mathematics.

Scientists and mathematicians, by contrast—particularly researchers who are not fearful that their religious beliefs will be undermined (either because they do not have any to begin with or perhaps because they have come to understand science and religion as occupying two "non-overlapping magisteria")—may be of the opposite opinion: a God-of-the-gaps science cannot help but foster an investigative sluggishness and ultimately become a "science-stopper."[10] A God-of-the-gaps mentality will affect researchers' motivation for pursuing open questions, espe-

---

9. Dembski suggests that a "supernatural" cause (or design) could be a legitimate, *scientific* inference to draw if probabilistically neither law nor chance was able to account for some given phenomenon.

10. See Plantinga, "Methodological Naturalism?"

cially one that may have adverse consequences upon deeply held religious beliefs. It would effectively dissuade scientists from relentlessly searching for natural explanations, meaning that there may be natural explanations for things that we prematurely ascribe to the supernatural.

According to this line of thinking, any willingness—even the faintest expectation—to find supernatural phenomena within nature can lead to the calling off of scientific and mathematical inquiries in areas where we simply do not know what the answers will be. How would one distinguish between a *reluctance* to find a natural cause for a particular event and an inability to find one? Furthermore, the prospect of not having an explanation *now* does not necessarily increase the prospect of *never* finding one. The reality of the matter may be that we just do not know. But if a religious researcher is convinced beforehand that God has acted supernaturally, the investigative threshold for that experimenter will be undermined by her prior beliefs. Another consideration is that there is no reason to suppose that God always acts in ways that must be inscrutable to science.

American philosopher John Dewey once quipped, "Two radically different reasons, however, may be given as to why a problem is insoluble. One reason is that the problem is too high for intelligence; the other is that the question in its very asking makes assumptions that render the question meaningless."[11] TS may prove a danger to science when, at the prompting of religious expectations—triggered by the wonder and grandeur of nature—it psychologically predisposes researchers to misidentify a problem as insoluble when it is actually only a problem of extremely high difficulty. So states Dewey: "To idealize and rationalize the universe at large is after all a confession of inability to master the courses of things that specifically concern us. As long as mankind suffers from this impotency, it naturally shifted a burden of responsibility that it could not carry over to the more competent shoulders of the transcendent cause."[12] Dewey feared that traditional Christian beliefs had caused the American public to abdicate its sense of intellectual responsibility. But what about responsibility to God and to upholding our traditional beliefs in him?

---

11. Dewey, *Influence*, 15.
12. Dewey, *Influence*, 17.

A curious feature of TS is its openness to "epistemological supernaturalism."[13] In many cases, TS can help convince people that what they know about the world through religion can be believed with utmost certainty. They can believe without having any doubts that a sacred event of one kind or another happened *supernaturally*. They may base their belief on revelation or accept it on the basis of religious experience. However, if a researcher were to adopt a supernatural epistemology, she will form the belief that all future research must *confirm* what she already knows on the basis of revelation. Once this happens, no amount of evidence will be sufficient to prove otherwise; all semblance of objectivity will be lost.[14]

A religious researcher who proceeds under the auspices of supernatural epistemology appears to be methodologically confused. One way to respond is to complain that science and mathematics do not leave room for God, but according to Palevitz, "It's not that science excludes God so much as it has no way of dealing with the concept."[15] Once God is admitted into the discussion, science ceases to be science. Religious writers like to point out that if there is no widely accepted definition for science as a discipline, then how can one say what it is not? However, if a scientist were to do science based on a supernatural epistemology, then that scientist would be ostracized by the broader scientific community. In one sense, at least, when we say that "science ceases to be science" we might mean, "scientists cease to work according to the methods agreed upon by scientists."

Whether a science carried out on the basis of supernatural epistemology can still be called science is not the only concern. Religious people also wrestle with the fact that religion, too, can become the subject to scientific and mathematical investigation. Many believers whom I have spoken with feel that religion and theology should be the ones investigating science, not the other way around. If one were to ask, "Which discipline should defer to other disciplines whenever there is a discrepancy?" religious people would likely say that science and mathematics should be the ones to adjust in response to religious claims. And this makes sense. If a religious believer adopts a supernatural epistemology and sees that the broader scientific and mathematical communities accept natural

13. Griffin, *Religion*, 13.

14. The philosopher of science Karl Popper once complained that virtually *every* theory can be confirmed if one looks for confirmations.

15. Palevitz, "Science," 175.

explanations for a particular event or phenomenon that she infallibly "knows" to be supernatural, she will discount the other communities' findings on supernatural grounds. Now admitting that one was wrong is not usually a pleasant experience (even for naturalists) but if a person *cannot be wrong*, how much less resistant will she be to admitting she was in error.

The fear of finding error can cause religious believers to look upon science and mathematics with suspicion—especially when they are left to their own devices and carried *outside* the parameters of religious control beliefs. Suspicions are compounded when some science and math writers announce that they can disprove religious claims. There is no shortage of religious beliefs that have proven false over time. From claims that the New Testament was written in an unattested "language of the Holy Ghost" to claims that fossils cannot possibly be remains of now extinct species since God is an efficient and effective Creator; any number of religious beliefs has given way to the findings of researchers.[16]

But what of the religious believer? What options remain for her? When the broader scientific community shows that the earth is almost a million times older than six thousand years of age, what is a person with a supernatural epistemology to do? The options seem rather limited: 1) insist that science is wrong; 2) insist that though the revelation is right, its interpretation is wrong; 3) claim that both the revelation and the scientific accounts are complementary (perhaps by integrating parts of each or suggesting that neither account gives a total description); or 4) admit the revelation may have actually been wrong in this particular case. Interestingly enough, all four responses can be made compatible with a commitment to TS.

It does not follow, however, that TS is insuperable. Over time, a jarring cognitive dissonance can set in. All the while, MN repeatedly proves its methodological fruitfulness in contemporary research. A growing number of results obtain under the auspices of MN and these results survive relevant attempts at refutation. Without privileging scientific and mathematical knowledge *per se* over against knowledge gained in other fields, MN gains in acceptance and validity in a way that TS cannot. Insofar as MN does not draw inquiry to a close and insofar as it allows for

---

16. This is not to suggest that scientists have not themselves made embarrassing claims during the course of their theorizing. The point is that their hypotheses are always subject to criticism and can theoretically be overturned.

findings to be corrected, MN is able to prove itself time and again as suitable for conducting research.[17] Even religious believers have to admit this. As Clarke observes, "it may be that questions which now seem almost beyond conjecture may one day be conclusively settled."[18]

MN and TS, then, seem to be at odds in their opposite expectations for research, and their competing views are not confined to science and mathematics. For this reason, some religious people are suspicious of any scholarship that does not leave room for the agency of spiritual beings. MN comes across as a metaphysical presumption that discounts religious beliefs right off the bat. With so much at stake, religious believers are not ultimately interested in how the rationale for MN is maintaining practitioner's motivation for pursuing specific lines of inquiry and holding them intellectually accountable. For some, it becomes part of their religious calling to defend religion against naturalism.[19]

---

17. This is different from saying that MN is a fruitful research *program*.
18. Clarke, "Credo," 185.
19. This paper was presented at the annual meeting of the Society for the Study of Religion, Nature and Culture, held in Morelia, Mexico, January, 2008.

8

Thoughts on the intermediate value theorem and the "knowledge-boundary" problem

IN THIS CHAPTER, I wonder if we can help address a philosophical problem by applying what is taught in a first semester of calculus. In his article on fallibilism in the *Internet Encyclopedia of Philosophy*, Stephen Hetherington suggests that "we have found a persistent problem of vagueness confronting various attempts to revise [the thesis that knowledge is justified true belief]. This might have us wondering whether a complete analytical definition of knowledge that p is even possible."[1] Hetherington argues in another place that if philosophers are unable to locate an epistemological boundary for knowledge, then they will have a "grounds for doubt" for the existence of a boundary.[2] In what follows, I propose that the way "boundaries" are handled in a first semester calculus class may suggest that the presence of vagueness Hetherington describes does not necessarily lead to a knowledge boundary problem.[3]

In each of his arguments, Hetherington takes a similar line of reasoning, namely, that if philosophers are not able to progress in their understanding of a question, the limitation probably lies with the question being asked rather than a shortcoming on the part of philosophers.[4] By claiming that epistemologists cannot know a knowledge boundary exists because a boundary between knowing p and not knowing p cannot be found,

---

1. Hetherington, "Fallibilism." The variable "p" represents any given proposition.

2. See Hetherington, "Boundary Problem," 42, where he explains: "It is the epistemological problem of knowing what is the maximum degree of fallibility that is allowable in knowledge's justificatory component."

3. Knowledge is supposed here to be "justified true belief."

4. Compare Sorenson, *Pseudo-Problems*.

Hetherington exploits borderline cases that often arise as puzzles when a person tries to claim a thing belongs to one category or another. For example, Hetherington remarks that "most epistemologists remain convinced that their standard reaction to Gettier cases reflects, in part, the existence of a definite difference between knowing and not knowing." Hetherington takes issue with the fallibilist claim that there's a strict difference between knowing and not knowing and argues that such a claim ultimately endangers knowledge itself. His argument seems to proceed as follows:

1) Fallibilists say that people either have knowledge that p or they do not.

2) Fallibilists, then, claim to know that there is a boundary between knowing that p and not knowing that p.

3) Fallibilists must cross a knowledge boundary in order to go from not having knowledge to having knowledge.

4) But epistemologists are not able to locate such a boundary.

5) A failure to locate such a boundary is a ground of doubt regarding its existence.

6) Therefore fallibilists "do not know there to be a justificatory boundary between knowledge and non-knowledge."[5] →← (Contradiction)

Conclusion: "[A]nyone who lacks knowledge of knowledge's having a justificatory boundary might well also lack knowledge of knowledge's even existing in the first place."[6]

Hetherington complains that if fallibilists hold that either an individual knows p or they do not, there is no allowance for degrees of knowing in terms of a more or less partial knowing regarding p and that these make better sense of how people come to knowledge.

Hetherington urges fallibilists to revisit the question of how to decide whether some belief p has enough justification to count as knowing p. What objective threshold can be decided upon to adjudicate in every case at precisely what point a belief p obtains sufficient justification to qualify it as knowledge? Philosophers given to thinking about matters of epistemic justification have not been able to agree amongst themselves as to how to

---

5. Hetherington, "Boundary Problem," 46.
6. Hetherington, "Boundary Problem," 47.

describe the knowledge threshold. BonJour and Hetherington agree that there is a knowledge boundary problem. The boundary for knowledge is not discernible. And if a boundary for knowledge cannot be found, it may very well not exist, or at the very least, may be an unfruitful way of construing knowledge. For if we cannot say we know where a knowledge boundary is located, then we cannot say we know that we have knowledge. And if we cannot say we know that we have knowledge, then we cannot say we know that knowledge is possible. And if we cannot say we know that knowledge is possible, we still can't say we know that knowledge is *not* possible. Along these lines, Hetherington remarks in his *IEP* article:

> The threats of vagueness we have noticed in some earlier sections of this article might be a problem for many epistemologists. Possibly, those forms of vagueness afflict epistemologists' *knowing* that a difference between knowledge and non-knowledge is revealed by Gettier cases. Epistemologists continue regarding the cases in that way. Are they right to do so? *Do* they have that supposed knowledge of what Gettier cases show about knowledge?[7]

Such problems regress in such a way as to affect every fallibilist claim. For at what point can one say that one knows *p*? Or again, at what point can one say that one knows the answer to the previous question? And at what point can one say that one knows the answer to *that* question? Here is the epistemological regress, one that not all philosophers take equally seriously.[8] Some epistemologists regard skepticism as *the* position to beat; others consider skepticism to be a threat of negligible magnitude.[9] Either way, the thesis that a measure of doubt regarding the location of a knowledge boundary implies a ground for doubt for the existence of a knowledge boundary is not immediately obvious. To show why, let us take a look at how in a first semester calculus class we come across scenarios that seem analogous enough.

---

7. Hetherington, "Fallibilism."

8. See, for example, Moser, *Philosophy*. Philosophy's "dialectic," as he calls the regress, compels BonJour to re-espouse internal foundationalism as the best response. See BonJour and Sosa, *Epistemic Justification*.

9. Williams helpfully distinguishes between "epistemological questions" and "epistemology" to explain why not all philosophers are interested in the perpetual threat of skepticism. See Williams, "Epistemology." For additional suggestions as to what skepticism accomplishes for epistemology generally, see Williams, *Unnatural Doubts*; and Stroud, *Significance*.

Thoughts on the Intermediate Value Theorem

There are at least three theorems that come to mind: the Intermediate Value Theorem (IVT), the Extreme Value Theorem (EVT) and Rolle's Theorem (RT). Each guarantees that when specific minimal conditions are met, some kind of threshold must be crossed even if that threshold is not immediately discernible. Consider, for example, IVT:[10] "Let f be continuous on a closed, bounded interval $[a,b]$, and let y be any number between $f(a)$ and $f(b)$. Then for some input c between a and b, $f(c) = y$." IVT indicates nothing with regard to what that number c might be, but it guarantees that whatever y one can imagine between $f(a)$ and $f(b)$, there will always be at least one number c that will yield $f(c) = y$.

Again, consider EVT: "Let f be continuous on the closed bounded interval $[a,b]$. Then f assumes both a maximum value and a minimum value somewhere on $[a,b]$." Nothing here is implied with regard to precisely what those values might be; the theorem merely establishes that such values will invariably exist. Both a minimum and a maximum must be *somewhere* inside $[a,b]$.

Lastly, RT: "Suppose that f is continuous on $[a,b]$ and differentiable on (a,b) and that $f(a) = f(b)$. Then, for some c between a and b, $f'(c) = 0$." Once again, the theorem says nothing about what this point c will ever be; it only upholds that it invariably exists.

It seems to me that each of these three theorems illuminates the likely inconclusiveness of Hetherington's argument strategy. Let us begin by clarifying that it would be wrong to interpret Hetherington as inquiring into the ontological status of these and other types of abstract boundaries when he suggests that the knowledge boundary does not exist. If a number theorist is in the process of creating an algebra and defines an additive inverse to have such and such properties, when she goes on to demonstrate that such a thing exists—and even that the inverse is unique—the claim is not to some ontological status *per se*, but something more like a methodological reassurance that additive inverses are indeed worth talking about.

In a similar way, Hetherington's talk of the existence of a knowledge boundary is not meant to draw attention to some ontological status that it may or may not possess but rather to suggest that the boundary in question is not a helpful way to speak of knowledge. In other words, Hetherington is saying that if epistemologists lack knowledge of the boundary's categorical instantiation, then they will have gained a ground for doubt

---

10. For the following theorems, see Ostebee and Zorn, *Calculus*.

in the boundary's existence, where "doubt in the boundary's existence" means "doubts regarding the fruitfulness of a boundary metaphor for knowledge."[11]

Perhaps fallibilists can co-opt the intermediate value theorem to help them escape Hetherington's clutches. Each of the three theorems referenced above claims that under certain circumstances un-discerned points can still be known to exist, even if we don't know where. Perhaps of the three theorems, IVT can provide us with the clearest illustration (see Figure 1 below).

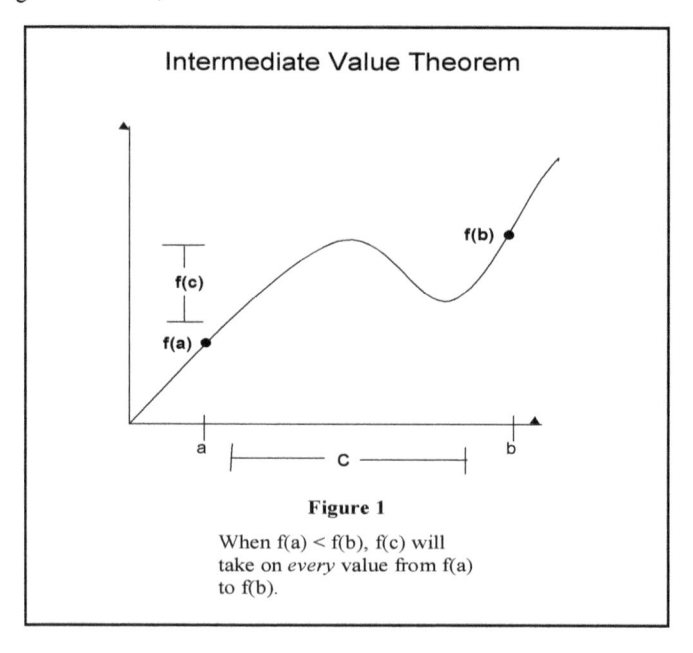

Intermediate Value Theorem

Figure 1
When f(a) < f(b), f(c) will take on *every* value from f(a) to f(b).

In order to make the analogy convincing, one would need to import an appropriate analogy for continuity and also persuade others that a closed and bounded interval is involved. Accordingly, fallibilists might consider the relation of epistemic justification to epistemic states (knowing p and not knowing p) graphically and determine whether it can analogously exemplify a continuous graph on a closed and bounded interval. For if the epistemic justification interval is closed and bounded and if the relation between epistemic justification and knowledge is continuous, then a knowledge boundary can be said to exist irrespective of whether fallibilists can say much more about where the boundary is.

11. See, for example, Hetherington, *Good Knowledge*.

Thoughts on the Intermediate Value Theorem

The bounds of epistemological states that correspond to differing amounts of epistemic justification seem to range *from* a belief *p* so dissimilar epistemically from knowing *p* that it only obtains when one has the lowest possible epistemic justification for *p to* knowing *p* by virtue of an overabundance of epistemic justification. The *farthest* that one can be epistemically from having knowledge is presumably that epistemic state where one does not have any justification whatsoever for some belief *p*. So the lower bound of the interval is set at having near zero epistemic justification for *p*. Conversely, the *closest* one can come epistemically to having knowledge is presumably that epistemic state where one has precisely that amount of justification that qualifies knowing *p* as knowledge. With respect to an upper bound, it turns out to be the case that all epistemic states that correspond to amounts of justification *greater* than that needed to initially achieve knowledge, such as epistemic states that result from having an overabundance of epistemic justification, amount to the constant, as it were, of knowledge. Thus the upper bound can reasonably be set as any amount of epistemic justification that *exceeds* that minimal amount necessary for knowledge. Each of the amounts of epistemic justification that acts as a bound for the analogous interval is conceivable; it seems the necessary condition of a closed and bounded interval could be plausibly met. (A suggested graph for this scenario is given in Figure 2.)

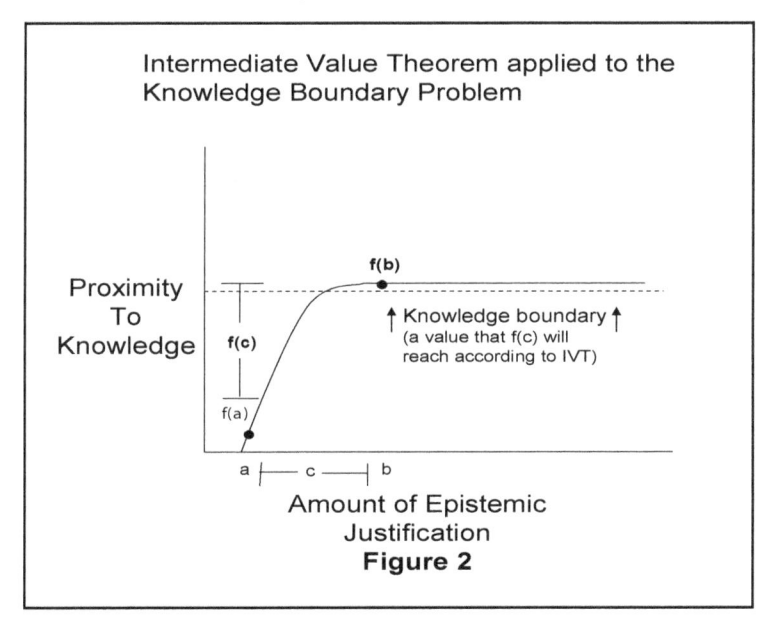

Intermediate Value Theorem applied to the Knowledge Boundary Problem

Proximity To Knowledge vs. Amount of Epistemic Justification. Knowledge boundary (a value that f(c) will reach according to IVT).

Figure 2

79

But how about continuity? In calculus, a function is said to be continuous wherever
$$\lim_{x \to c^-} f(x) = \lim_{x \to c^+} f(x) = f(c).$$
Translated into epistemic terms, one might say that if it is the case that increasing epistemic justification has the exact opposite effect to epistemic status than the decreasing of epistemic justification has with regard to knowing p, then the limit as epistemic justification approaches c has an analogical property of continuity when it is related to knowledge. In terms of inputs and outputs, the input variable would be the epistemic justification at hand and the output variable a corresponding epistemic distance, as it were, from knowing p. In an attempt to avoid a "non-absolutist" account of knowledge, the minimal amount of epistemic justification required for knowing p cannot be an endpoint if the interval is to have its intended analogical effect.

This can still be accomplished if the bounds set for the interval are not dictated by knowledge but rather by the amounts of epistemic justification at hand. Then the last thing required of us—to suggest an analogous account of
$$\lim_{x \to c} f(x) = f(c)$$
—seems to take care of itself since the proximity to knowledge that an amount of epistemic justification yields is precisely the proximity to knowledge that that amount of epistemic justification yields. Increasing epistemic justification has an opposite effect to epistemic status than decreasing epistemic justification by the same amount. In other words, the increasing and decreasing of epistemic justification from either side of the amount of epistemic justification in question will at each instance be equal to the amount of epistemic justification available at that instance and the amount of epistemic justification available at any instance will always be achieving the limiting proximity to knowing p. A belief moves closer to being knowledge with the addition of more epistemic justification and conversely becomes weaker—proportionately moving *away* from being knowledge—with the removal of that same amount of epistemic justification.

If IVT's conditions can be analogously met in this or some comparable way, the conclusion would seem to follow that there exists an amount of epistemic justification c such that $f(c)$ is knowledge *even though philosophers cannot say much with respect to what that amount of epistemic justification is.* Accordingly, ignorance with regard to the location of a knowledge boundary indicates nothing with regard to its existence. Then Hetherington could still be right to say that vagueness plagues a fallibilist's ability in identifying knowledge boundaries, but he would be wrong to suggest that this poses a real epistemological problem for fallibilists. The IVT may provide fallibilists a way conceptually to circumvent "the problem" of vagueness without being forced to somehow deny its otherwise puzzling effects.[12]

In this chapter, I mused whether math can be brought to bear on problems in philosophy, specifically a knowledge boundary problem in epistemology. Perhaps, the way we broach "boundaries" in first semester calculus can help shed light on a possible answer, or at the very least a better understanding of some of the difficulties being posed.[13]

---

12. Compare Hyde, "Higher Order."

13. This paper was presented at the joint meeting of the American Mathematical Society and the Mathematical Association of America, Washington, D.C, January, 2009.

9

On the associative property of addition and its application to the Godhead

COMMONPLACE IN CONTEMPORARY CHRISTIAN academia is the investigation of the advantage of a "Christian perspective" to such-and-such academic discipline and this-or-that academic problem. Practitioners of this reformational approach to general knowledge also have extended their line of inquiry to mathematics.[1] The converse application, however, is very seldom explored. Can there be any advantage to a "mathematical perspective" of Christian theology? Can mathematics inform theological problems? These questions may appear threatening to some and arcane to others, but a little creativity may deliver more than a mean theological yield. To date, those who have undertaken the integration of math and theology have produced mainly historical studies and excursions into cosmology. This paper endeavors to convince readers of the serviceability of mathematics for specific areas of theology proper.

Taking as an example a mathematical exploration of the Christian doctrine of God, I will show that math is able to enlighten theological discourse. The argument below propounds an inherent limitation upon our mathematical (or better, arithmetic) faculties. By introducing these limitations along with the generic nature of basic algebraic algorithms, we can gain certain insights into what the problem of the Trinity specifically entails. Many explanations have been given for the Church's inability to understand fully the doctrine of the Trinity. One Asian theologian "contextualizes" the doctrine, finding fault with the Greek logical axiom of noncontradiction, and posits that an Asian "both/and" type logic is better

---

1. See, for example, Howell and Bradley, *Mathematics*.

On the associative property of addition and its application to the Godhead

equipped to apprehend the doctrine. One Christian philosopher claims that it is because we lack appropriate conceptual categories to describe the triune God that we cannot fully explain him.[2] Neither claim delves deeply enough into the nature of the problem at hand.[3] The present paper aspires to a more precise explanation for the incomprehensibility of the Christian doctrine of God. While being mindful that the doctrine of God is sacred territory, I will argue that the binary limits of our arithmetic processes will forever keep humans from comprehending the Trinity. By integrating insights from theology, mathematics, and cognitive science, I will argue that humans' arithmetic capacity is designed in such a way that we cannot cognitively assimilate the historic doctrine of the Trinity.

Belief in the Trinitarian God of Christianity and in the incarnation of the second person of the Trinitarian God is what distinguishes Christianity from every other religion. If these two inseparable doctrines are relinquished, then Christianity reduces to simply one of myriad forms of expression of the human religious impulse. The orthodox creeds, then, are of singular importance to Christianity. The "Athanasian" Creed has been said to entail at least the following propositions:

---

2. Respectively, the conclusions of Lee, *Trinity*, and Davis, *Logic*. Interestingly enough, it seems that not a few evangelicals are open to a "both/and" claim like the one Lee offers. For instance, in his explanation of the relationship between the Old and New Testaments, Goldsworthy writes: "It is generally recognized that the relationship of the two Testaments is one aspect of the unity and diversity . . . within the canon. . . . This is one form of a philosophical and theological issue which underlies all attempts to understand reality: the relationship of the one to the many, of unity to plurality." He continues: "While the natural tendency is to solve these problems by allowing unity or diversity to dominate (an either-or solution), the Christian gospel suggests a distinctively Christian perspective embracing both unity and diversity (a both-and solution)." A problem arises, however, when he suggests a Christian pedigree for "both/and solutions" by appealing to Chalcedon: "The apostolic understanding of Jesus pointed to the mystery of the one person who was both fully God and fully human. It required a "both-and," rather than an "either-or" approach. Later the church formalized this perspective in the doctrine of the incarnation, and particularly in the formula of the Council of Chalcedon in AD 451." He adds: "*The doctrine of the Trinity is the epitome of 'both and' formulation. God is conceived as both one and many (three). The early heresies about God tried to define his being in ways that compromised either the unity of the three Persons or their distinctiveness* [emphasis added]." See Goldsworthy, "Relationship," 82–83.

3. Davis' observation concerning categories is right as far as it goes. Still, there seems to be more involved with Trinitarian parlance than a lack of appropriate categories. For the shortcomings of both Davis' and Lee's conclusions, see notes 16 and 17 below.

Ideas at the Intersection of Mathmatics, Philosophy, and Theology

1. The Father is God.
2. The Son is God.
3. The Holy Spirit is God.
4. The Father is not the Son and the Son is not the Holy Spirit and the Holy Spirit is not the Father.
5. There is one and only one God.[4]

Many have dismissed the above propositions as contradictory or unintelligible. For present purposes, we will presume the non-contradictory status of the above five statements.[5] It is the business of non-intelligibility that may find a few answers here. The charge of non-intelligibility means to say that even if the propositions are not formally contradictory, they do not contribute anything meaningful to one's understanding of God.[6] Non-intelligibility implies that the doctrine of the Trinity is so difficult or obscure that its content (whatever it is) is vacuous. I will argue that though the doctrine teaches an articulate, coherent reality (it is intelligible), Christians will always fall short of complete cognitive assimilation (it is not comprehensible). We will see that this failure seems to occur on account of binary tendencies in our innate process of collecting and combining individual objects and on account of the very nature of the arithmetic processes themselves.

The situation at face value is such that Christians assert that the Christian God is three-in-one and one-in-three. A simple way of trying to present such a belief in terms of numeric operations yields: $1 + 1 + 1 = 1$, where the first "1" represents the Father, the second the Son, the third the Spirit, and the fourth the total number of existing gods.[7]

---

4. Compare Feinberg, *No One*, 438, and Davis, *Logic*, 132–144.

5. What is the intended referent for "God"? Is it "The Father is not God as such; for God is not only Father but also Son and Holy Spirit," etc? Compare A. J. Augustus, *Systematic Theology*, 1.605. Similar questions arise regarding the function of "is," where predication appears to be in mind for (1), (2) and (3) but perhaps existence in (4).

6. It is important to remember that Christians do not believe these five statements on account of logical inventiveness or theological imaginativeness, but precisely because they believe them to be revealed by God in Scripture. Since these statements are believed to be a part of God's self-disclosure, it is no cause for alarm, in their view, that they should be accepted as mysteries.

7. Cartwright, *Philosophical Essays*, 187–200. In his chapter devoted to the problem of the Trinity, Cartwright refines Peter Geach's relative identity and reviews its aptitude when applied to Trinitarian language. Geach, for his part, sees a need to establish identity

On the associative property of addition and its application to the Godhead

There are at least two immediately obvious options open to the learner of arithmetic that would relieve her of this absurdity. The first and most obvious is to correct the sum by replacing the one with a three. Though this adjustment would satisfy arithmetically, when we recall the theological assertion that the arithmetic equation is supposed to represent, it is at once jettisoned as impermissible. The second option is to amend what lies on the opposite side of the equality symbol by emending the numerals in any number of ways. One suggestion that seems to commend itself is to reason that $1 + 1 + 1$ is not an entirely accurate representation because what the first "1" is, the second is also; what the second "1" is, the third is also. Therefore, given our peculiar circumstance, it is legitimate to rewrite the equation as $1 + 0 + 0 = 1$, since the second and third 1's are the same as the first. In other words, it is not technically the case that we have three different 1's here, but the same 1 repeated three different times. Thus, it is not right to say we have three because in the end, there is only the one and same 1.[8] The ground covered here, albeit in a grossly simplistic manner, has shown with what ease one can arrive at the ancient opposite errors of (1) polytheism and (2) monarchianism. *The situation at face value is such that Christians assert that the Christian God is three-in-one and one-in-three.*

To maintain our bearings in what follows, it might prove helpful to rewrite these twin perils in alternate forms that would include other possible formulations of the same unorthodox scenarios. Let us say, then, that if any formulation can be reduced to either of the following two formulas, then they have ceased to reflect the historic Trinitarian confession. Accordingly, we will remember:

---

in relation to a specific "something": "X is the same so-and-so as." What follows attempts to build upon Geach's ideas. I first learned of Geach's application of relative identity to the Trinity through the work of van Inwagen. Though I have not seen his name in the literature, it seems to me that the entire Christian tradition is heavily indebted to the medieval (dare I say patristic?) theologian Boethius (c. 480–524), for his work on the Trinity in his *Theological Tractates*. Boethius' discussions concerning identity with reference to the Trinity anticipate contemporary forays into relative identity.

8. If I call out for pizza three times in one night, though the pizzeria may in a sense say that it had three customers, the fact still remains that I am a single customer. Compare Russell: "When we say $1 + 1 = 2$, it is not possible that we should mean 1 and 1, since there is only one 1: if we take 1 as an individual, 1 and 1 is nonsense, while if we take it as a class, the rule of Symbolic Logic applies, according to which 1 and 1 is 1." See Russell, *Principles*, 135.

(1) $F + S + H = \Theta \longleftrightarrow \Theta \bmod 3 = 0$ or

(2) $F + S + H = \Theta \longleftrightarrow F = S = H$, where $F + F + F = F$.[9]

Moreover, F, S, and H can signify only one of an object.[10] In other words, we are ruling out the possibility that F can be a sum of more than one object. Therefore, F = 2 oranges cannot be true; F can only be one of whatever it is that F is and likewise with S and H. The same, however, cannot automatically be said to hold for Θ since it is F + S + H by definition. Indeed, the task at hand is to make this hold for Θ also without lapsing into (1) or (2).

In the case that one has $x + y + z$, it is only possible to simplify the expression if one variable can be rewritten in terms of another[11] or, better still, if all three of the variables could be rewritten in terms of a fourth. Perhaps, the latter strategy can prove serviceable. Let F be an apple, S an orange, and H a pear. F + S will not reduce to anything but an apple and an orange respectively. We can recognize the two objects separately, but we lack a linking variable to conjoin them (i.e., we cannot say we have two apple-oranges). Still, if there existed a fourth variable that could hold F, S, and H in common, we might be able to progress a bit. Let us rewrite F, S and H in terms of a fourth variable Π. (Normally, a new variable v, for example, would be introduced such that $v = 2x + 5$, $y = 5v$ and $z = v^2$ and the like in order to manipulate x, y and z in terms of v. For our purposes,

---

9. Readers who are mathematicians may be uncomfortable with the use of "+" here. They are free to substitute "□," "◊," and the like, understanding that we are considering an abstract commutative and associative operation for the sake of illustration. For the benefit of non-mathematicians, the ordinary "+" symbol has been retained. Equations (1) and (2) are, after all, mock trials with real addition. See note 15 for a brief rationale for the use of "+" and further on in the paper, where I discuss the nuances between "+" and "and" in more detail, especially with respect to the Father, Son, and Spirit relations I am proposing.

"x mod n" is the operation under which x is divided by n with or without remainder. For example, "100 mod10" is 0 since 10 divides 100 without remainder. In the same manner, "101 mod10" is 1 since 10 divides 101 with remainder 1. So $\theta \bmod 3 = 0$ would indicate that θ is divisible by 3. It is the duty of this formula (1) to detect a form of polytheism, namely "tri-theism." The "mod" function was chosen because it facilitates future qualifications with minimal revision.

10. As hinted at above, the variables were chosen with the following in mind: F denotes the Father, S the Son, H the Spirit and θ God. However, initial trials will involve other substitutions.

11. This line of inquiry does not seem promising since to express the latter two variables in terms of the former is what got us to (2) in the first place.

On the associative property of addition and its application to the Godhead

we must unfortunately trade these quantities for a conceptual analogy to this standard algebraic algorithm. Instead of the algebraic expressions [2x + 5, etc.], we will call upon various categories [e.g., fruit], as described by Aristotle, for example.[12] Let Π, therefore, denote any type of fruit. Now it appears that Π can rightly be substituted for any of F, S or H. Hence, F + S + H = Π + Π + Π = 3Π. So we have moved along to the following:

(1a) 3Π = Θ ← → Θ mod 3 = 0 or

(2a) 3Π = Θ ← → Π = Π = Π, where Π + Π + Π = Π.

On account of our substitution above, it seems that (1a) is unavoidable and (2a) is impending, if we overreact to the threat of (1a). (1a) *is* inevitable if Θ is divisible at all.[13] Fruit, as we have constructed it, is divisible, and it is evident that we have not only three types of fruit, but three individual fruits. Θ (whatever it is), in other words, is three and not one, divisible into three "smaller" parts. Θ, for us, is the number of gods that exist; there is only one divine substance. The Christian faith, however, holds that God is indivisible; he is utterly simple. Or is he?

Gregory of Nazianzus wrote: "For they are divided without division, if I may say so; and they are united in division." Gregory confesses that he speaks of a paradox, but we must explore the paradox a little further to accomplish our goal. The Cappadocian Father must have meant, among other things, that "God is divisible in a way that is different from the way

---

12. This has no noticeable effect on the argument since it is the nature of the operation itself (or any operation for that matter) and not the quantities employed that are later called upon to argue my point. The coefficients are what interest us here. An infinite number of combinations would provide the desired coefficients. For example, x = 2v, y = v and z = 0 yields the target 3v = q. The description of F as being only one of whatever F is does not nullify these types of substitutions. Even if it did, the myriad that take the form F = ½v + 9, S = 2v − 1 and H = ½v − 8 and the like accomplish the desired result. The ambiguous function of the equals symbol will be discussed briefly below.

13. Θ has intentionally been left undefined. What Θ might be need not detain us here, at least, as far as the fruit analogy goes. It is without the limits of this essay to rehearse the long journey to the final formulation of the Christian doctrine of God. Briefly, for us, 3Π will refer primarily, *but not exclusively*, to "three realities and three persons" and Θ will refer primarily, *but not exclusively*, to the divine *ousia* (substance). The equations aim to approximately depict the whole Godhead. It is agreed that every analogy of the Trinity falls short of that which it purports to represent. Each variable here should technically include the substance and the persons since, though the substance and the persons can be distinguished, they cannot be separated. It is only for the sake of the argument that one side of the equation focuses on the persons and the other on the substance. For the phrase "three realities and three persons," see Stead, *Divine Substance*, 241.

that he is indivisible, and he is a unity in a way that is different from the way that he is divisible." This is quite a mouthful, but it is an important mouthful nonetheless. The significance lies in the implication that there are different "ways" to God. But before inquiring of these different "ways," it is appropriate to remember that "we can speak of simple things only as though they were like the composite things from which we derive our knowledge."[14] It is only on account of our frailties that we must conceive God in such complexity. In reality, he is utterly simple.

If there are different "ways" to God (i.e., the ways in which he is divided are not the same ways in which he is united), then it becomes apparent that the relation that obtains in our formulas is not strictly accurate. Not only is the relation (=) inaccurate, but the operation (+) may be also. Nevertheless, we will continue to employ the operation while qualifying the relation. When a Christian affirms that $3\Pi = \Theta$ (that F, S and H are the one God), it may be the case that the Christian considers God to be three in ways that are different from the ways in which he is one. In other words, $3\Pi = \Theta$ is not an adequate rendering of the theological confession. When one writes ½ = 2/4 = 3/6 , etc., one is expressing the fact that each term refers to the same exact quantity. For our purpose (for better or for worse), we have lapsed from quantities to categories, but the same relation is implied by the "=" symbol we are using at present. $3\Pi = \Theta$, therefore, might be understood to convey that 3Π and Θ refer to the exact same category (and not necessarily quantity), yet this is contrary to the orthodox description. The matter can be set in bolder relief by realizing $3\Pi = \Theta \longleftrightarrow 3\Pi - \Theta = 0$ must be true if the equals symbol signifies its normal "equal quantity" relation. With equal *quantities*, the difference is always zero. Can it likewise be said that if you were to subtract the *category* "substance" from the *category* "person" that the result would be zero?[15]

---

14. Aquinas, *Sum. Th.* 1.3.3.1. For Gregory, see *Orat. 5, On the Holy Spirit*, 14.

15. Herein lies the reason for opting for an arithmetic or algebraic analogy and not one solely based upon symbolic logic and set theory as is commonly done by philosophers. Discussions that incorporate set theory into analyses of the Trinity (e.g., those that search out the implications of Relative Identity) tend to obfuscate the nuances that distinguish equality (and there are several headings under equality) and identity. Perhaps, attempting to answer questions of equality before establishing different kinds of identity amongst the persons of the Godhead would further illuminate the exact nature of the paradox. I am willing to admit a certain degree of inadequacy in the arithmetic alternative presented here (for starters, it is not "purely" arithmetic), but the perceived

On the associative property of addition and its application to the Godhead

We are already familiar with this problem. Earlier we saw that we could not add one apple and one orange. The same would be the case if we sought to subtract one orange from one apple; we are forced to hold the tension between the two objects without reducing them to one type. In order to continue, we saw that we must search for another variable in terms of which the others could be expressed. Thus, we are forced to keep the "persons" and the "substance" in tension without reducing one category into another, for no extant category will ever become available for useful deployment. This is the impasse of the mystery beyond which humans cannot progress. Still, it is well known that by using mathematics, humans can sometimes proceed beyond that which would ordinarily impede us.[16]

Some readers may be of the opinion that we have abandoned our quest too hastily and that $3\Pi = \Theta$ or $F + S + H = \Theta$ should be revisited. Surely other possibilities abound, but, as mentioned above, it is not the varied possibilities that are of interest. It is the *operation* that merits

---

inadequacies by no means invalidate its didactic utility. Arithmetic and logic have fuzzy bounds; the activity of one is very often the activity of both. Variables in algebra, after all, often stand for bare mathematical concepts (e.g., "real number") and, for all intents and purposes, not for a hypothetical set of discrete quantities (e.g., $(-\infty,\infty)$). A preponderance of algebraic work abstains from discrete quantities altogether. The same can be said for the "+" sign as well. The "+" sign, at times, can be a "stand-in" for any other operation that a practitioner can imagine (assuming it is commutative and associative). For this reason, the conclusion of the present argument, in my judgment, survives unscathed. For a similar view concerning the use of concepts and operations in algebra, see Sawyer, "Algebra."

16. In this case, mathematics may prove especially useful by exploring the realm of "what if?" If a pertinent category does exist or will exist in the future, we will not be able to employ it in order to reduce the tension. Such employment will either collapse into (2a) above or simply return us to our initial point of departure at the beginning of this essay. For example, let us imagine that a satellite in the near future is able to transmit an ultraviolet photograph of a physical relation (infinitesimally high-speed electrons or what have you) that obtains within the sun that no scientist has encountered to date or has ever even thought possible. Let it be supposed that they assign a category, "*f*abric *warp*" or some such name, to encapsulate the essence of the phenomenon. If we were to posit that "*f*abric *warp*" is such a category that it were to categorically subsume both "person" *and* "substance," we may try to substitute in fw as follows for each: $3fw = fw$ (or $fw + fw + fw = fw$, which is, of course, (2a)). This is no help at all, and is, in fact, worse than $3\Pi = \Theta$, for it leaves us with an absurdity since its single solution is "zero." For this purpose, Davis' observation above (that we lack the categories to proceed any further), though revealing, is not definitive, for even if we did have the categories, they would not afford resolution.

scrutiny. Revisiting the formulas will lead invariably to (1a) or (2a), and the reason for these outcomes lies in the operations involved. It should be clear that every restatement of the "Athanasian Creed" can be expressed in either of these forms:

(3) $3\Pi = \Theta$ or

(4) $F + S + H = \Theta$.

Since (4) is the commonest, it will occupy our attention from here on out.[17]

As we have implicitly surmised above, "Father *and* Son *and* Holy Spirit" is not technically the same as "Father *plus* Son *plus* Holy Spirit." The concept behind the word *plus* has the intrinsic connotation of bringing together the objects under consideration (whether abstract or concrete) and combining them in such a way that there appears a "new" object (the sum). By contrast, to simply "*and*" objects together means to collect the objects in question without necessarily combining them in any particular way. In other words, the collecting stops short of combining (i.e., there is a mere collection in the end and not a sum). The "obvious" meaning of *plus* is notoriously difficult in that it is not always clear how the "new" object relates to the initial objects prior to their being "*plus*-ed." Fundamentally and non-trivially, it is at least understood that the whole is greater than its parts.[18] Inherent in this relation is a notion of

---

17. Once again, the objection might be raised that the divine substance is not merely the three persons of the Godhead considered collectively, but is a substance itself and not a combination of persons. In other words, the divine substance exists *alongside* the persons so that what is really taking place is this: $F + S + H + Đ = \Theta$, where Đ is the divine substance and Θ is the Trinitarian God. The objection is noteworthy, even if the "arithmetic" representation of it is quite problematic. (Incidentally, Lee's "both/and" approach in *The Trinity in Asian Perspective* seems to fall prey to the error of this equation. His contextualized "Asian" Trinitarian God is, unfortunately, nothing but a *quaternium quid*.) The objection has force because Christians recognize a distinction between substance and person and between person and person. However, if Θ is the whole Godhead (i.e., the Christian Trinitarian God), Θ is not simply substance, but the whole God. We must remember that the Đivine substance is essential to each variable—it is not only essential to Θ, but also to each of F, S, and H. In other words, what is intended by $F + S + H = \Theta$ is more accurately reflected by $FĐ + SĐ + HĐ = Đ (F + S + H) = \Theta$. This alternate form, however, was judged to be too cumbersome for an essay of this length. It is hoped that the simpler equation will suffice to present analogously the point that is being made.

18. It is arguable that there may be times when the result of a *plus* will be no different from that of an *and*. When this occurs, one can claim that no *plus* ever really took place or that the nature of the objects was such that the *plus* did take place but that it did not have its usual effect on the objects. A similar scenario arises in discussions concerning

On the associative property of addition and its application to the Godhead

measurement, and not only measurement, but also a *method* by which one is able to ascertain a measurement. Both the method and the resulting measurement normally require spatial and temporal considerations including density, locality, velocity, temperature, span, height, weight, form, and so on. Even when dealing with abstractions, corresponding abstract equivalents to measurement and method obtain; a similar mental process along a suitable calculus is used. It is this very act of "measuring" that occurs prior to, during and after *plus*-ing that proves inadequate when applied to the Trinity.

The phrase "during *plus*-ing," aside from its awkward construction, may come as a surprise to some. Is there really a "during *plus*-ing" phase to adding one plus one? A child is given one animal cracker and then another. Immediately, it is obvious to her (whether she can articulate it or not) that she no longer has one but two. Prior to *plus*-ing she had only one cracker; subsequently she had two. Whence this "during *plus*-ing" stage? That is just the problem. Practically speaking, when adding one plus one (or anything at all), there is no "during *plus*-ing" stage. One may object that when a student adds 27 + 18 and resorts to scrap paper in order to affect the computation, he is experiencing the "during *plus*-ing" stage, but this is not true. The busy student only *appears to experience* the "during *plus*-ing" stage with the help of his stationery aids. We must not confuse the time taken or the materials used with the actual act of *plus*-ing.[19] Though the entire computation may take a student five or ten seconds, real *plus*-ing takes (or better, lasts for) but an instant. "Seven plus eight is fifteen" is the first act of *plus*-ing involved in the given exercise. Or if the student resorts to the bane of his tutor—counting on his fingers—he will proceed: "Seven. Eight, nine, ten . . . fifteen!" Thus we have eight instances of *plus*-ing to accomplish the first step of the exercise.[20]

---

the relations between classes or sets and their terms. For example, is a set just its members or something more? For a critical discussion on a set's relation to its terms, see Lucas, *Conceptual Roots*, 311–39.

19. Recording the numbers, crossing out digits, "carrying," etc. are only preparation for each of the instances where the student actually brings the two numbers together mentally and comes away with his sum. After all, ". . . mathematical notation no more *is* mathematics than musical notation is music . . . It is in its performance that the music comes alive; it exists not on the page but in our minds." The same can be said of math (which Devlin does say in the sentences that follow). See Devlin, *Math Gene*, 9.

20. For good measure, lest anyone begin to worry, it should be noted that the following does not apply to adding machines, computers and the like because a programmed

Ideas at the Intersection of Mathmatics, Philosophy, and Theology

What possible relevance does this have for the Trinity? It is pertinent in every way. The crucial feature that precludes a more comprehensive understanding of the doctrine of the Trinitarian God lies in the *measurement* process (utilized by all humans) mentioned earlier. Granted, it is not "seven plus eight" with which Christian believers must wrestle constantly, but with a situation that is actually much simpler and very similar to "*one plus one plus one*." This is not to claim that God is linear or piecemeal, but rather that the measurement process which humans instinctively apply to all objects is the same in both "seven plus eight" and "one plus one plus one." *It is this very act of "measuring" that occurs prior to, during and after plus-ing that proves inadequate when applied to the Trinity.*

The measurement process that I have in mind is akin to what Brian Butterworth calls "numerosity."[21] This term refers essentially to cardinal numbers. Determining numerosity (i.e., determining exactly how many of something there are) requires the ability to specify individual objects and then to organize them into a collection. These abilities are innate; some scientists are now arguing that infants along with many different types of animals possess a sort of "number sense."[22] This innate sense is limited to distinguishing among one, two, and three of a given thing. More specifically, I have in mind what I call the *pairing mechanism*. In their study, Lakoff and Núñez have posited a "pairing capacity" whose function it is to match a person's count to the corresponding object in a given collection since the count must be distinguished from the collection of objects.[23] The *pairing mechanism* propounded here, by contrast, is the process by which a person pairs an already counted item (or a cumulative sum) with the next item to be counted. Whereas Lakoff and Núñez are concerned with the pair that has one member in a source domain (object collection) and a second member in a target domain (arithmetic), I am concerned with relating a pair of objects that are both within the same domain (be

---

abacus does not *experience* anything! In a similar vein, rote memorization is discounted for it circumvents the very process upon which we are attempting to focus. If one objects that everyone counts from memory, we need only substitute an unfamiliar multiple (counting by three or eight, etc.) to find an analogous operation. If that still fails to satisfy the objector, he will still agree that counting does at least demonstrate the use of a pairing mechanism (see below).

21. Butterworth, *What Counts*, 10.
22. See Dehaene, *Number Sense*.
23. Lakoff and Nuñez, *Where Mathematics*, 51.

On the associative property of addition and its application to the Godhead

it source or target). In other words, instead of focusing on the "cognitive mechanism that enables us to sequentially pair individual fingers with individual objects" (speaking of counting on one's fingers),[24] I am focusing on the mechanism that pairs two individual objects (or a running sum and an individual object or even two running sums) together in order that they might then be combined or *plus*-ed. The best example of what is meant here is the algebraic explication of the associative property of addition: $(a + b) + c = a + (b + c)$.

Notice that the only difference between the two sides of the equation is that different pairs are set apart by parentheses. The function of the two sets of parentheses is to signify which two terms are meant to be combined first each time. It matters not whether one adds $(a + b)$ and then c (as on the left) or first adds $(b + c)$ and then a (as on the right). The two sums will be equal. These parentheses signal the reader to pair terms in a particular manner. The process that the parentheses describe is the *pairing mechanism* set forth here.

Pairing and *plus*-ing are not the same action. Pairing is logically first, even if in simple cases they seem to obtain simultaneously. In order for any *plus*-ing to occur, objects (concrete or abstract) must first be brought "together," organized or *measured*.

The pairing mechanism is an inherently binary operation. I posit that it can only operate on a single pair of objects at any given time (whether the pair consists of two single objects, a collection considered jointly as a single collective and a single object, or two collectives). Though operations many times give the appearance of being far more complex, it will always be the case that it can be reduced to the repeated organization of pairs of objects if carried out by humans. Multiple examples of this can be found in the algorithm known as the order of operations. To arrive at a solution or an equivalent expression of a given expression, if a choice exists as to which operation should be applied first, one must work through parenthesis first, then exponents, then multiplication, and so on. Algebraic expressions of virtually every sort must be approached with this algorithm.

Consider $5 \cdot 3 + 4 + 5 \cdot 7 - (2 \cdot 2 \cdot 2)^2$. All operations here are binary; only two numbers can be "operated on" at a time. Every act of "combining" is at its most fundamental level the exercise of the pairing mechanism.

---

24. Ibid.

Within the parenthesis, for example, we have three two's being multiplied $(2 \cdot 2 \cdot 2)$. One with a familiarity with these types of exercises may simply count the two's and know from memory that $2^3 = 8$, but recall that memorization circumvents the actual operation. The analogy will not hold for rote memorization since memorization is more an act of association than combination.[25] However, if one approaches the parenthesis by means of the operations themselves, he would combine two of the two's $((2 \cdot 2) \cdot 2)$ and then combine the product (4) with the last two to get a final product $(= 8)$.[26] The same holds for $15 + 4 + 35$: two numbers would be paired together and that sum then would be added to the third. The pairing mechanism is inherently binary, which may explain why most (I would argue all) operations are also binary. Thus, mathematics has been used to uncover an implicit limitation within many (if not all) mental gathering processes.

These tacit processes extend to Christian discourse as well. For example, a theological corollary to the natural employment of an innate "pairing mechanism" is that if God demonstrates a plurality of any sort, humans would automatically consider a duality first and then proceed from there. In other words, a bi-une God is easier to recognize than a tri-une one. This is precisely what has happened historically. Both the Father and the Son were soon recognized as somehow being God, where the Father was not the Son and the Son was not the Father.[27] The precise nature of their relationship (or at least what their relation was not) took centuries to establish before moving on to consider a third divine person, the Holy Spirit.[28] I think that the proposed pairing mechanism contributed in large measure to the order of theological discovery. The reason that the early

---

25. To the degree that counting is performed from memory, the analogy seems to weaken because it involves more of an associative capacity (associating one entity with another and recognizing an ordered relationship between numbers) than a faculty for combining (one combined with one is two, two combined with one is three). Nevertheless, the pairing mechanism can then be identified with Lakoff and Núñez's "pairing capacity." To reiterate, counting from memory circumvents the *plus*-ing operation, but requires some sort of pairing. Counting by other multiples than one may prove analogous.

26. The same holds for "shortcuts." If the shortcut circumvents the operation entirely, it is back to memorization. Many shortcuts, though, inevitably proceed through the required operations, only at some simpler level.

27. See, for example, Hurtado, *Origins*, 63–98.

28. For these and other developments, see Kelly, *Early Christian Doctrines*.

On the associative property of addition and its application to the Godhead

church first wrestled with the relationship between the Father and the Son and then that among the Father, Son, and the Holy Spirit is because the early church leaders were limited by the pairing mechanism. If it is unclear how the pairing mechanism would help us better *understand* a bi-une God, minimally, we can say that it causes us to *recognize* a bi-une God more easily. Insofar as the pairing mechanism assists us in recognizing a bi-une God, it would assist us in understanding him. By definition, however, the *binary* pairing mechanism offers no assistance whatever in recognizing our *tri*-une God. To the extent, therefore, that it hinders us from recognizing our God, it is an impediment to our understanding him.

We have suggested above that most operations are binary, or at the very least, that they are approached as if they were on account of the employment of a pairing mechanism. We will now apply these observations to the earlier discussion of the Trinity. (4) $F + S + H = \Theta$ is the equation with which we will resume.

It was surmised that, based on categorical failures, there existed an impasse beyond which we could not explore. A new problem that emerges is that the pairing mechanism that we naturally and necessarily employ as an early step in combining objects is fundamentally inadequate for the present task. The inherent binary nature of the pairing mechanism does not have the range for the Trinitarian formula. It is not enough to combine F and S and then consider $(F + S) + H$. Nor will $F + (S + H)$ or $(F + H) + S$ suffice. The Patristic idea of perichoresis, or the interpenetration of the Father, Son and Holy Spirit, prohibits each of these isolated combinations.[29] In fact, the only combination that is consistent with perichoresis is $(F + S + H)$, and this at once ceases to be the essential grouping of pairs. Therefore, it is not only a categorical failure that stands in the way, but also an operational failure. The operation needed here is one that acts upon three objects simultaneously, but it is one with which we are unfamiliar, and (based upon the binary limitations that have been placed on our pairing mechanism) may be one that we cannot discover or invent or, in the least, properly perform. If this is the case, it follows that we are unable to combine $(F + S + H)$ in a single stroke for it is without our binary parameters. Hence, we can expect our descriptions of the Trinitarian God of Christianity to be necessarily either broad and vague—and in many ways inexplicable—or inaccurate and erroneous, as were those espoused

---

29. See Prestige, *God*, 282–300.

by the heretics. The *plus*-ing that Christians need is one that involves the gathering of triples and not that of pairs. If what I have argued is true, then the intercourse between mathematics and theology has discerned an inestimable hindrance to the appreciation of the doctrine of the Trinity.

Furthermore, the binary restriction is not the only problem that humans face in understanding the Trinity. A salient feature of the *plus*-ing operation itself, beyond its binary approach, is not able to mirror the relations of the Trinity. Above, a distinction was made between *plus*-ing and *and*-ing. Whereas the former involves a sum that subsumes the objects that were considered separately prior to the operation, the latter does not always result in a sum. The sum is a collective entity that considers all objects together without reference to their individuality. It was also pointed out that there are three phases to *plus*-ing: before-, during- and after-. The after- phase will have obtained whenever a sum is apparent and the individual objects are not. The before- phase includes all that is done in preparation for the calculation of a sum (i.e., when individual objects are present and the sum is not). The during- phase was defined as that instant when *plus*-ing actually occurs. The problem was that a during- phase never really seems to exist. The final connection to make here is that in order to conceive properly of the Trinity, we must recover that during- *plus*-ing stage. That is, we should seek out the instant when the objects under consideration are no longer merely individual objects but are not yet a full sum either. Rather, they are neither individual objects (strictly speaking) nor a sum. This is the closest we can come to the idea of interpenetration.

In other words, (F + S + H) needs to be combined as a triple (not by pairs) in such a way that they are *plus*-ed, but the combining process must freeze itself in the during- stage.[30] That elusive moment when (F + S + H) is combined must be preserved in a "snapshot" and not allowed to pass by, else the sum will formally result and the individuals will disappear. The measurement of (F + S + H) at that precise moment would allow for a more faithful understanding of the Trinity.[31] However, such precision

---

30. (F + S + H) with parenthesis (as opposed to without parenthesis) means to signify the all-at-once-ness of the original F + S + H. The parenthesis will serve to remind us that it will not do to add from left to right or in any other binary way; rather, an immediate measurement of the triple is required.

31. As already mentioned, I am not at all convinced that this dilemma is forced upon us by "either/or" logic or solely by a lack of appropriate categories. The dilemma is caused

is a perennial chimera. Alas, in the end, it may be the case that a certain amount of illusion lies at the foundations of arithmetic.[32]

To sum up, there is no real problem with the doctrine of the Trinity. The doctrine is neither contradictory nor nonintelligible. The Christian church has effectively articulated the doctrine of the Trinity in her creeds; the reality described is a legitimate one that involves no contradiction. Still, Christians (and non-Christians for that matter) do and will continue to have problems with the doctrine of the Trinity. It describes a wondrous God whom we cannot cognitively assimilate. The human arithmetic capacity is designed in such a way that its tendencies account for a significant part of why the historic doctrine of the Trinity cannot be properly appreciated. This is due, it was argued, to the inadequacy of a binary pairing mechanism that humans inevitably employ when contemplating the three persons of the Godhead. Moreover, the moment in which the

---

by the fact that God is three in a way that we cannot fully appreciate. The dilemma is caused by the fact that there is no way for us to "freeze" the during *plus-* ing stage in order to observe or experience how a combination can obtain that comes after a mere gathering of objects, yet before the final sum. The snapshot must be of a time when F, S, and H combine with each other in such a way that: if one were to look for F, one would find that S and H inhere in F; if one were to look for S, that F and H inhere in S; and if one were to look for H, he would find that F and S inhere in H. Such an operation would be unique, but it seems that the operation could not exist within time. It is time that causes *plus*-ing to have a prior to, during and after phase. The fact that all operations are performed "in time" causes the result to have the lasting influence. But if the analogy presented here is in many ways valid, it appears that it is the process itself, or the actual act of *plus*-ing as we have termed it, that is the dimension of the operation that would need to obtain as a constant, long-lasting reality. And this is impossible "in time." An act endures for but a moment (or for an indefinitely short span, as some would argue), but this act would need to endure for an eternity (or, at the very least, endure for long periods of time at the command of an individual perceiver). It is not a repeated act that will do here or a long act comprised of many smaller ones, but one act performed at one time that obtains continuously throughout time. For this to be achieved it seems that it would have to be performed "outside" time; moreover, in order to view it, one would also have to do so from "outside" time. Of course, I digress too much; the metaphysics of time is a fascinating and perplexing study in its own right.

32. Compare Frege, *Foundations*, 35: "I distinguish what I call objective from what is handleable or spatial or actual. The axis of the earth is objective, so is the centre of mass of the solar system, but I should not call them actual in the way the earth itself is so. We often speak of the equator as an *imaginary* line; but it would be wrong to call it a *fictious* line; it is not a creature of thought, the product of a psychological process, but is only recognized or apprehended by thought." It may be the case that arithmetic itself, though not a "creature of thought," is similarly only recognized by thought but not fully apprehended by it.

actual operation obtained proved elusive. The conclusion was drawn that even with the expansion of the pairing mechanism to an equivalent that worked with triples, the nature of the *plus*-ing operation itself fails to accurately reflect the nature of the Trinity. Therefore, humans will always have a problem understanding the Trinity.

These conclusions were couched within the contours of a broader argument that proffered the usefulness of mathematics for theology proper. The analogy presented above, for example, can be applied to both the economic and imminent Trinities insofar as the latter is revealed in the former.[33] An imaginative and careful mind should be able to find other creative ways to incorporate mathematics into theological discussions.[34] The present exercise was an attempt at such incorporation: an algebraic exposition of the Christian doctrine of God. In due course, legitimate obstacles were identified that reflect inherent limitations upon simple, everyday operations. Obviously, this is not to say that these limitations are the *only* reasons that the Trinity remains incomprehensible or that an algebraic analogy was the *only* way to isolate these features. Nor has it been claimed that mathematics can "solve" the problem of the Trinity. Suffice it to say that a "mathematical perspective" can prove quite useful to Christian theologians, even if it only plays a negative role (as it did here). So, without being impious, the next time someone asks, "Can any good thing come from mathematics?" we should give more credence to the reply, "Come and see."[35]

---

33. For an overview of the issues that pertain to the various views, see O'Carroll, *Trinitas*, 94–6. I consider the economic Trinity to be an ontological "subset" of the immanent Trinity, but not a proper one.

34. For example, devise an analogy that attempts to illustrate the divine perichoresis.

35. This paper was prepared for a course on the "Doctrine of God" at Westminster Theological Seminary, Philadelphia, and subsequently published as "Pairing and Plus-ing the Godhead: An Algebraic Analogy," *Perspectives on Science and the Christian Faith* 55 (2003): 166–174. Used by permission.

10

Remarks on the search for an infinite God in the philosophy of Edmund Husserl

PHENOMENOLOGY HAS RECENTLY TAKEN a "theological" turn. One of the main reasons for this turn is the work of Jean Luc Marion. His re-conception of the transcendental subject as given, gifted and convoked has spurred on some very interesting discussion. Provocative parallels have been intimated by Marion and others between Judeo-Christian conceptions of a creator God and the metaphysical notion of infinity. Yet there is still another area of philosophical inquiry where Marion has had considerable impact: Cartesian studies. During the course of his researches on Descartes, Marion has discussed in great detail how Descartes follows the lead of several Christian philosophers when describing God as infinite. Claiming that God is fundamentally infinite, for Descartes, is to say something positive about God, according to Marion. In what follows, I suggest that the same fundamental association of infinity with God that Marion finds in Descartes also shines through the work of Edmund Husserl, who looked with great interest at Descartes' meditations while developing his own self-styled philosophy.

There is a case to be made to the effect that certain strands of Christian thought have contributed both to Husserl's original motivation for doing phenomenology and to Husserl's insight regarding what aspect of Christian conceptions of God lends itself most naturally to the formulation of a rigorous, scientific philosophy. I argue that Husserl's way of framing the phenomenological question of the infinite horizon of absolute consciousness may have been suggested to him by Christian theology, if not directly, then indirectly via developments in mathematics. It is not coincidental that a new mathematical understanding of infinity is gaining considerable attention precisely when Husserl first begins writing philosophy and that the man responsible for this new conception was very interested in things theological.

For my part (and, if I am permitted to read between the lines, on the part of Marion), I cannot help but expect to see a deliberate, meta-metaphysical search, as it were, for the Judaic-Christian God at the heart of the Husserlian project. Yet since Husserl himself forswore that he should never be talked about as if he were a Christian philosopher,[1] a connection between Husserlian phenomenology and Christian ruminations about an infinite creator God can profitably be sought within the context of specific conceptual puzzles that had come to light in the discipline that influenced Husserl the most, mathematics. Husserl himself concedes as much: the fundamental catalyst for his phenomenological project was religion—a religion, he says, that was somehow able to bear the existential brunt of the mathematical problems that occupied him at the time.[2]

In what follows, I argue that the infinite horizon that opens up to the *ego* upon the performance of the *epoche* is properly extrapolated by Marion to describe an "originary" encounter with God.[3] To support this, I point to how Christian philosophers have historically held a position conceptually tantamount to Cantor's idea that there are greater and lesser degrees of infinity. But even more important than that is the historic Christian understanding that the concept of infinity ontologically points to a fundamental aspect of God *that is uniquely ascribed to him*.[4] I argue that Husserl's discovery of the absolute ground of the world is precisely what Marion indicates: a transcendental, phenomenological glimpse of the *infinite* Creator of the world.

In the fifteenth century CE, Nicholas Cusanus began musing that human observations (along with a number of other experiences) are perspectivally conducted; thus they cannot possibly be as objective as they naturally and initially appear to us. In his first philosophical treatise, *On Learned Ignorance* (1440), Cusanus applies this radical epistemological

1. Jagerschmid, "Conversations."
2. See Husserl, *Shorter Works*, 360.
3. Marion observes that to call the other that primally convokes the subject, God, merely gives a name to the problem and does not resolve much. For some of the developments in phenomenology that prepare the way for Marion's theological extrapolations, see Taminiaux, *Metamorphoses*, and Moyn, *Origins*.
4. More recently, process theologians have embraced the idea of a finite Christian god.

Remarks on the search for an infinite God in the philosophy of Edmund Husserl

discovery to cosmological considerations, drawing the conclusion that the cosmos must be in at least some sense infinite:

> However, it is not the case that in any genus—even [the genus] of motion—we come to an unqualifiedly maximum and minimum. Hence, if we consider the various movements of the spheres, [we shall see that] it is not possible for the world-machine to have, as a fixed and immovable center, either our perceptible earth or air or fire or any other thing.[5]

Cusanus' argument certainly throws into question the possibility of a geocentric model of the cosmos, but even more importantly the argument suggests that since the motion of heavenly bodies admits no unqualifiedly maximum or minimum points, the universe itself cannot have any physical center. A fixed center can only be ascertained relative to unqualifiedly maximum and/or minimum boundaries, but since neither of these can be definitively established (since a point farther or closer in distance than a suggested boundary can always be posited), the former cannot be found either—the former depending on the latter two and vice versa:

> Hence, the world does not have a [fixed] circumference. For if it had a fixed center, it would also have a [fixed] circumference; and hence it would have its own beginning and end within itself, and it would be bounded in relation to something else, and beyond the world there would be something else and space (*locus*). But all these [consequences] are false. Therefore, since it is not possible for the world to be enclosed between [a physical] center and a physical circumference, the world—of which God is the center and the circumference—is not understood. And although the world is not infinite, it cannot be conceived as finite, because it lacks boundaries within which it is enclosed.[6]

It is interesting to note that although Cusanus ascribes the characteristics of infinity to the cosmos, he explicitly states that the world is not infinite. After all, the only infinity that can be philosophically and theologically admitted is God—and Cusanus admits as much when he claims that God is both the center and circumference of an apparently infinite cosmos. Cusanus is very careful to point out that the world is finite, even if it cannot be conceived as finite. It cannot be infinite for only God is infinite.

5. *On Learned Ignorance*, II.11, cited in Harries, *Infinity*, 46. The bracketed material is supplied by Harries.
6. Cited in Harries, *Infinity*, 47.

Ideas at the Intersection of Mathmatics, Philosophy, and Theology

Compare Rene Descartes' remarks in a letter to Henry More (February 5, 1649):

> In my opinion, it is not an affected modesty on my part, but a necessary caution, to say that some things are indefinite rather than infinite. I understand God alone as being positively infinite. I confess that I do not know in the case of other things—such as the extension of the world, the number of parts into which matter is divisible, and similar things—whether they are or are not absolutely infinite. All I know is that I am not aware of any limit to them and therefore, from my point of view, I call them indefinite.[7]

Blaise Pascal is another Christian thinker familiar with the infamous "double infinite." In his *De l'esprit géométrique*, after commenting upon the fundamental interrelatedness of motion, number and time, he muses: "Thus there are properties common to all things, and the knowledge of them opens the mind to the greatest wonders of nature. The principle one includes the two infinities which are found in all things, infinite largeness and infinite smallness."[8] In another place he explains that "[t]hese extremes touch and join by going in opposite directions, and they meet in God and God alone."[9] Even if infinites can be found in every corner of the cosmos, so much so that "human reason does not want to abstain from giddying itself about them,"[10] God will always remain the only true infinite.

That there are *demonstrably*, different kinds of infinity is Georg Cantor's revolutionary proposal. Although discussion of the specifics of Cantor's work would certainly take us too far afield, Cantor's work can be theologically interpreted as mathematical evidence for an infinite/indefinite distinction. In fact, such an interpretation is urged upon Cardinal Johannes Franzelin by Cantor himself when the theological implications of his theory of transfinite numbers come under the scrutiny of Catholic philosophers. Franzelin takes Cantor's lead when he clarifies:

> Thus the two concepts of the Absolute-Infinite and the Actual-Infinite in the created world or in the *Transfinitum* are essentially different, so that in comparing the two one must only describe the

---

7. Taken from Descartes, *Meditations*, 171.
8. Cited in Blay, *Reasoning*, 7.
9. *Pensées*, fragment 199, cited in Blay, *Reasoning*, 8.
10. Galileo's phrase, cited in Blay, *Reasoning*, 9. Blay cites a number of scientists who observe that the infinite is ultimately incomprehensible even though our minds cannot resist pondering it.

> former as *properly infinite*, the latter as improperly and equivocally infinite. When conceived in this way, so far as I can see at present, there is no danger to religious truths in your concept of the *Transfinitum*.[11]

Implicit in the Christian understanding of infinity is, among other things, the concept of measurement, and according to William of Ockham in his *Quodlibetal Questions*, measurement can be taken in at least three senses: "(i) [S]ome measures are measures through replication, e.g., an ell, (ii) some are measures through containment, e.g., a peck of wheat, and (iii) some are measures through perfection and similarity."[12] Ockham maintains that God-talk is mainly interested in infinity with regard to perfection and not spatial or numerical infinities, yet it is important to remember that for the metaphysician the transition among Ockham's three realms of the infinite is a seamless one even if mathematicians, logicians and others today might dismiss it as illegitimate.[13] According to Descartes, the human understanding of God is such that he is without limits of any kind. The limitlessness of God is something humans confidently assert in a positive way. On the other hand, "in the case of other things, our understanding does not in the same way positively tell us that they lack limits in some respect; we merely acknowledge in a negative way that any limits which they may have cannot be discovered by us."[14] Thus, although multiple infinities seem to abound, God is the only true infinite.

In his study of Descartes, Marion recognizes that the "fundamental concepts" involved in Cartesian metaphysics led post-Cartesian metaphysics to the thesis that "the freedom found in the *ego* follows from the infinity of its will, which itself depends on its likeness to God."[15] This is precisely the theme that can be discerned in Husserl's writing.

For example, Cantor's foray into infinite sets raises a host of questions for Husserl—so much so that Hill can remark: ". . . it [is] easy to believe that [Husserl's] crisis was aggravated, if not actually induced by Cantor's bold experiments with mathematics and epistemology."[16]

---

11. Cited in Dauben, *Georg Cantor*, 146.
12. 7.18, reply to the main argument. See Ockham, *Quodlibetal Questions*, 656.
13. See Moore, *Infinite*.
14. Cited in Blay, *Reasoning*, 10.
15. Marion, *Metaphysical Prism*, 278.
16. Ortiz Hill and Rosado Haddock, *Husserl or Frege?* 146.

Ideas at the Intersection of Mathmatics, Philosophy, and Theology

Merleau-Ponty broaches one facet of the problem in his course notes on "Husserl at the Limits of Phenomenology, 1959–1960" when he asks, "But can we reactivate everything? In fact, it is impossible (the individual and even a cultural group have finite capacities of reactivation) . . ." He rehearses the Husserlian objective in his class notes as "the removal of limits from our capacity, in a certain sense its infinitization."[17] It should come as no surprise, then, that Husserl himself squarely sets the blame for the preponderance of human naivety in philosophy upon the discovery of the infinite:

> The historical course of development is prefigured in a determined way by this attitude toward the surrounding world... Quite rapidly, a first and great step of discovery is taken, namely, the overcoming of the finitude of nature already conceived as an objective in-itself, a finitude in spite of its open endlessness. Infinity is discovered, first in the form of the idealization of magnitudes, of measures, of numbers, figures, straight lines, poles, surfaces, etc. Nature, space, time, become extendable *idealiter* to infinity and divisible *idealiter* to infinity. . . .
>
> What effect did the intoxicating success of the discovery of physical infinity have on the scientific mastery of the spiritual sphere? In the attitude directed toward the surrounding world, the constantly objectivistic attitude, everything spiritual appeared as if it were [simply] spread over [the surface of] physical bodies. Thus the application [to it] of the natural scientific way of thinking seemed the obvious thing to do.[18]

Husserl's historical account is perceptive: it is upon the discovery of the infinite that the mathematization of the surrounding world ensues and eventually turns inward upon the subjectivity of humanity.[19] "But," explains Husserl, by doing this, "the researcher of nature does not make clear to himself that the constant fundament of his—after all subjective—work of thought is the surrounding life-world; it is always presupposed as the ground, as the field of work upon which alone his questions, his methods of thought, make sense."[20] The intentional subject is presupposed by every

---

17. Merleau-Ponty, *Husserl*, 65.

18. "The Vienna Lecture," included as Appendix I in Husserl, *Crisis*, 293.

19. Compare Rózsa Péter's narrative in *Playing with Infinity* on the replacement of geometrization with mathematization on account of the problem of the infinite.

20. Husserl, *Crisis*, 295.

"work of thought" and thus cannot properly be the subject of a natural investigation.

Husserl goes on to postulate that there are parallel infinites corresponding to various physical infinites within subjective experience. By so doing, Husserl opens up the problematic of infinity to the phenomenological investigation of consciousness. Yet he insists that phenomenology is the only appropriate way for infinity to be investigated. Husserl's talk of an intentionality of infinites refers not to the direction of human intentionality to physical infinites and it is not merely a manner of speaking. His interest lies primarily in researching and affecting anew historical moments of spiritual transformation within which humanity's intentional direction is reoriented in such a way that it becomes more and more attuned to the cultural manifestations of its universal subjective structures. He writes:

> Ideas, meaning-structures that are produced in individual persons and have the miraculous new way of containing intentional infinities within themselves... With the first conception of ideas, man gradually becomes a new man... Within this movement at first... there grows a new sort of humanity, one which, living in finitude, lives toward poles of infinity.[21]

Husserl's ambitious claim is that Western civilization has the potential (and has had this potential since "the first idea," i.e., the advent of Greek philosophical thought) to transcend humanity's natural finitude and redirect its intentional regard toward the infinity that resides within itself, i.e., toward the infinite horizon of humanity's own collective consciousness. He explains: "Precisely in this way there arises a new type of communalization and a new form of enduring community whose spiritual life, communalized through the love of ideas, the production of ideas, and through ideal life-norms, bears within itself the future-horizon of infinity: that of an infinity of generations being renewed in the spirit of ideas."[22] Thus for Husserl, there are not only physical infinities, but also subjective infinities that philosophy can properly and rigorously investigate. Thus we observe with Tasíc that Husserl seems to posit the "life-world" precisely

---

21. Husserl, *Crisis*, 276–77.
22. Husserl, *Crisis*, 277.

Ideas at the Intersection of Mathmatics, Philosophy, and Theology

as an ahistoric, atemporal *continuum* upon which to ground the infinite diversities of all the experiences of consciousness:[23]

> No other cultural shape on the historical horizon prior to philosophy is in the same way the same sense a culture of ideas knowing infinite tasks, knowing such universes of idealities which as a whole and in all their details, and in all their methods of production, bear infinity within themselves in keeping with their sense.[24]

Yet it is not any philosophy that allows for the possibility of escape from finitude. Only *scientific* philosophy opens infinity up for contemplation in such a way that an infinite horizon of spiritual tasks and ideals becomes fully available to consciousness. In this context it is helpful to remember that Husserl's life-long project is to restore a lost sense of rigor to philosophy and science. Science, in the usual sense of the word, is understood by Husserl to refer to a synthesis of "the original natural attitude" and "the theoretical attitude" in an incessant "process of finitization."[25] Positive science, according to Husserl successfully achieves knowledge of the "things of the world" but never knowledge of the "true being of the world." This is because for the positive sciences the world is "pregiven"; "the world is the constant presupposition." The goal of phenomenology, by contrast, is to push behind human subjectivity to "discover the absolutely functioning subjectivity," "the subjectivity which objectifies itself" in order to gain the knowledge of the universal structures of consciousness, allowing for a rigorous reexamination of the world that can only be carried out in light of discoveries made possible by transcendental phenomenological reductions.[26]

Husserl does not hesitate to liken transcendental reduction to religious conversion. The existential redirection of one's intentional regard such that a shift is affected from the natural attitude via the performance of a reduction to a transcendental, phenomenological investigation of the life-world *and vice versa* is likened to an experience that closely resembles religious conversion. Husserl reminds the reader that one "should remember what we learned before about the phenomenological reduction as a reorientation of the natural mundane attitude. We can return from

23. Compare Tasić, *Mathematics*.
24. Husserl, *Crisis*, 279.
25. Husserl, *Crisis*, 283.
26. Husserl, *Crisis*, 261–262.

Remarks on the search for an infinite God in the philosophy of Edmund Husserl

the reorientation into the natural attitude . . ."[27] Of course, this reminder does not serve only to bring to mind that one *can* return to the natural attitude but that one *should* return from the reorientation of the reduction to the natural attitude refreshed, or even afresh and radically anew. The end of the phenomenological reductions is precisely to "return to the natural attitude" with a newly acquired perspective and appreciation for the absolute "ground of the world."[28] An assemblage of Husserlian confessions exemplifies precisely what this suggests with regard to my proposed connection between phenomenology and Christianity.

According to Husserl, philosophy should be undertaken with the following teleological aim:

> The straight and necessary path [philosophers] must take allows them to see only one side of the task, at first without noticing that the whole infinite task of theoretically knowing the totality of what is has other sides as well. If inadequacy announces itself through obscurities and contradictions, this motivates the beginning of a universal reflection. Thus the philosopher must always devote himself to mastering the true and full sense of philosophy, the totality of its horizons of infinity.[29]

And for Husserl, philosophy properly undertaken implicates itself as ultimately religious:

> Only when the nature of a transcendental consciousness is understood, can the transcendence of God be understood. Thus all religion has been naïve and therefore unintelligible, but in the phenomenological attitude the naïve theses of religion receive not only intelligibility, but also a certain validity, as do the naïve theses of our experience of nature, or of anything else. The ethical-religious questions are the last questions of phenomenological constitution.[30]

Husserl's phenomenology has an inherently religious ethos:

> God and God's word, man in search of God, living as a child of God, and so on—all of that will acquire a new and richer meaning

---

27. Husserl, *Crisis*, 258.
28. Husserl, *Crisis*, 260.
29. Husserl, *Crisis*, 291.
30. Husserl, "Conversation with Husserl and Fink, 24/11/31." See Cairns, *Conversations*, 47.

> for you as soon as you have developed a sensitive eye for history, and—and this is not far removed from it—a sensitive eye for an absolute contemplation of being, as well as for a contemplation of the "world" from the viewpoint of pure subjectivity.[31]

In his studies on Descartes, Marion has occasion to discuss the connection made by Christian thinkers between how the infinite is "inherent" to the ego and how the infinite is fundamental to God. It is interesting that Husserl should have these anticipatory remarks regarding phenomenology generally:

> Perhaps it will even become manifest that the total phenomenological attitude and the *epoche* belonging to it are destined in essence to effect, at first, a complete personal transformation, comparable in the beginning to a religious conversion, which then, however, over and above this, bears within itself the significance of the greatest existential transformation which is assigned as a task to mankind as such.[32]

Husserl privately expresses his spiritual interpretation of his own phenomenological project in the following words:

> We find a way to God. The unsearchable Within.
> The absolute world and God as the one 'substance,'
> As the source of all being,
> As the principle of all development in the world,
> As the world-ordering power, as world-creator . . .[33]

There is indeed a connection to me made between phenomenology as the search for the infinite God.

I have set out an argument above that approaches Marion's interpretation of Descartes on the import of the concept of infinity for Christian philosophy. As a transcendental encounter that by means of reductions obtains an "originary" glimpse of the infinite Creator of the world, phenomenology exhibits similar interests. Suggestive comparisons can be made between Husserl's appropriations of the infinite horizon—an infinite that somehow exceeds that of physical infinites—and that order of infinity that in Christian theology can only connote God. Both Marion and Husserl would surely agree: by their very nature the phenomenological

---

31. Husserl, *Shorter Works*, 362.
32. Husserl, *Crisis*, 137.
33. Cited in Hart, "Précis," 158.

reductions entail a return to the natural attitude from the sphere of reductive bracketing. However, the return is one that is overwhelmed by a new immanence of "crisis." Yet perhaps the phenomenological reductions are also meant to lead one to a greater meditative appreciation of the infinite horizon, an intimate and apprehensive escape from finitude, a transcending of the transcendental subject, and not least, a groping for the infinite God.[34]

---

34. This paper was presented at a philosophy conference on "The Philosophy of Jean-Luc Marion" held at the Franciscan University of Steubenville, April, 2008.

11

Observations regarding the Kalam argument and its disavowal of actual infinites

IN THE COURSE OF their very instructive book, *Theism, Atheism and Big Bang Cosmology* (*TABC* hereafter), William Lane Craig and Quentin Smith touch upon whether an actual infinite can exist. Craig argues that an actual infinite cannot exist in the physical world because its existence would lead to a number of practical absurdities. His argument takes the form of an indirect proof: "Suppose x *is* true, then the following absurdities follow. Therefore, x must be false." The premise that actual infinites cannot exist in the physical world is part of a larger argument:

A1. An actual infinite cannot exist.

A2. An infinite temporal regress of events is an actual infinite.

A3. An *infinite* temporal regress cannot exist.[1]

In the present chapter, I set out to do two things. First, after briefly recounting Aristotle's distinctions between potential and actual infinites, I try to contest the non-existence of actual infinites by suggesting various decimal scenarios as examples of where actual infinites might be said to exist (where some are somehow "contained" in the finite). My suggestion is that perhaps there is an intrinsic relation between the finite and the infinite such that the presence of the former does not always exclude the latter. I also explore Craig's examples of absurdity and ponder whether

---

1. Craig and Smith, *Theism*, 9. The argument is a sub-argument for the Kalam argument for the existence of God (*TABC*, 4):
   I. Everything that begins to exist has a cause of its existence.
   II. The universe began to exist.
   III. Therefore the universe has a cause of its existence.

there might be a need to distinguish between types of "existing." It seems to me that an important ambiguity might be present that may render A1 above mistaken or, at the very least, in need of further clarification. My overall purpose is not to argue that actual infinites do, in fact, exist—although this seems to me to be right—but rather that their existence is not to be ruled out metaphysically or philosophically on account of persisting, counter-intuitive paradoxes.

Craig cites Hilbert when he distinguishes an actual infinite from a potential infinite, explaining that an actual infinite is a "determinate totality"[2] and a potential infinite is an infinity that is never taken as a whole. Since at least as far back as Aristotle, it has been helpfully maintained that when it comes to the infinite, "the word 'is' means either what potentially is or what fully is."[3] According to Hilbert, the potential infinite exists and is not merely an abstract idea, but "the infinite in the sense of an infinite totality . . . is an illusion."[4] This distinction was made in antiquity and is crucial to Craig's argument. He insists these two senses must not be confused.

To illustrate the difference, let us imagine situations that would require the postulation of increasingly large numbers. There might be a computer that began to count a thousand numbers a second and was left to this task for twenty years. There could be a god who could travel a hundred thousand *yojanna* during a blink of an eye and travel at such speeds for six months at a time.[5] Extremely large numbers help us express great distances and quantities even when we cannot fathom their numerical immensity. Distances and quantities can presumably increase indefinitely at will. For this reason the word "infinite" (i.e., not finite) seems an adequate description. But can we ever have an instance when the infinite is present *as a totality*? Can we have a case where the infinite is wholly present in the circumstance at hand, an actual actuality, as it were?

---

2. Craig's phrase, *TABC*, 7; Hilbert uses "completed totality" and "infinite totality." See Hilbert, "Infinite." According to Aristotle (*Physics*, 3.5), what is "infinite in full completion . . . must be a definite quantity."

3. Aristotle, *Physics*, 3.6.

4. Hilbert, "Infinite," 184. On the following page Hilbert sees this as something that needs to be realized not only for the good of mathematics, but "for *the dignity of the human intellect* itself."

5. Approximately a million kilometers according to ancient Jaina traditions. See Joseph, *Crest*, 250.

In the two examples just cited, anytime a tally was to be taken, the number/distance that resulted would obviously be finite (even if very large). The potential for the infinite would always remain but only *if we were to keep going*. Enter the *potential* infinite. The *actual* infinite would require the totality and that would only obtain if the computer (or the god, to keep with the above examples) were never to stop. This sort of infinite, Craig argues, exists in our minds only, if they can be said to exist at all.[6] It would be one thing to say that one *could* keep counting or traveling forever, but it would be another thing entirely to say that they *did* forever keep counting or traveling—that they *have finished doing so* and that there is an actual, real-life number/distance as a result. The potential infinite can be accepted since at all times the "infinite" in question remains but a possibility; however, the actual infinite is an absurdity and, according to Craig, should not be thought to exist.[7]

When reading the debate in *TABC*, decimal numbers came to mind and whether they might be considered actually infinite, at least *in some respect*, even if many of them are regularly conceived as finite. Consider with me the somewhat surprising limit case of $0.\overline{9}$.

Let us think for a moment about the real number 0.9999999999 . . . In order to indicate that we have a repeating, non-terminating decimal in mind, convention dictates that the repeating digits be truncated and that simply $0.\overline{9}$ be written. If one were interested in rounding this number to any given place (i.e., any place less than the tens place), the result would invariably be 1.0.

This raises an interesting question: are $0.\overline{9}$ and 1.0 equal? The naïve answer seems to be that the two numbers are not equal to each other since $0.\overline{9}$ is precisely $0.\overline{9}$, an infinite succession of decimal 9s and not 1.0. Conversely, 1.0 is precisely 1.0 and not an infinite succession of decimal 9s. Although they are, no doubt, extremely close to each other in the quantities they express, the former cannot be reduced to the latter nor the latter to the former.

---

6. For his part, Craig argues that actual infinites are physical impossibilities. He has little patience for the transfinite "paradise" of mathematicians.

7. A full exploration seems to warrant investigating the roles time, tense and eternity might play in these discussions, which may be why Craig has done so much work on these topics. Although I have not read all of his work, I still wonder whether mathematical constructions of numbers have been taken into consideration for this question of the actual infinite.

Observations regarding the Kalam argument

A problem that arises with this line of thinking is that if it were the case that the two numbers are distinct, then one should be able to find some third number that is between $0.\overline{9}$ and 1.0. Put another way, what would their difference be if $0.\overline{9}$ and 1.0 are not the same number? It would not be $0.\overline{1}$—even if it seems that it should be—since adding $0.\overline{1}$ and $0.\overline{9}$ would not give you 1.0 back. It would give you $1.11111\ldots0$. Similarly the proposed difference would have to be $0.00000\ldots1$, but this too poses a problem since $0.\overline{9}$ means that there is no last 9 to which one can add the $0.00000\ldots1$. The proposed subtraction problem seems to be intractable when presented in decimal form. Does this mean that the numbers are equivalent? That conclusion cannot be made yet—at least, not without some more probing, for it may not be initially clear why the difference should be 0.

To illustrate what is happening here, let us consider arithmetic cases involving two infinitely repeating decimals along with their fraction representations. Presumably, 1.0 minus $0.\overline{3}$ is $0.\overline{6}$ since $3/3 - 1/3 = 2/3$, and $2/3 = 0.\overline{6}$. When expressed as fractions, the subtraction involving the repeating, non-terminating decimal does not pose a problem. $1.0 - 0.\overline{3} = 0.\overline{6}$ is the decimal equivalent of $3/3 - 1/3 = 2/3$, but, from one vantage point, it hardly makes any sense.

$1.0 - 0.\overline{3}$ cannot yield $0.\overline{7}$ because if you add $0.\overline{7}$ and $0.\overline{3}$ together you do not get 1.0. But still if you add $0.\overline{3}$ and $0.\overline{6}$ together, you do not get 1.0 either; rather, you get $0.\overline{9}$. And with this we are back to the original question.

Are $0.\overline{9}$ and 1.0 the same number? Writing the decimals as fractions strengthens the argument that $0.\overline{9}$ and 1.0 are the same number. In order to see this, let us consider the difference: $10/11 - 7/11 = 3/11$.

Written as decimals, we would have $0.\overline{90} - 0.\overline{63} = 0.\overline{27}$. Does adding the subtrahend and the difference seem to yield the minuend when added out infinitely (whatever that turns out to mean)?

Again, $20/21 - 17/21 = 3/21$ is the rational equivalent of $0.\overline{952380} - 0.\overline{809523} = 0.\overline{142857}$. What happens when we try to get repeating decimals to add back together? To take another example, if $1.0 - 0.\overline{809523} = 0.\overline{190476}$, does not $0.\overline{809523} + 0.\overline{190476} = 0.\overline{9}$?

It should come as no surprise that a number of professional and amateur mathematicians have had a fascination with representing numbers in creative ways that involved infinity.[8] One connection that is relevant here is the relation between rational numbers and repeating decimals.

For starters, it does not appear possible to express $0.\bar{9}$ as a rational number. The form of the rational number it should take seems readily apparent: the numerator would have an infinite number of 9s and the denominator a 1 as the first digit with an infinite number of 0's behind it. Yet it is not possible to express such values given our numerical conventions.

Still, notice how the rational number that has 1 as the numerator and 9 as the denominator yields $0.\bar{1}$ as a decimal. Notice further how the rational number formed by having 2 as the numerator and 9 as the denominator yields $0.\bar{2}$ as a decimal. This pattern continues.

In fraction form, adding 1/9 to itself nine times yields 9/9 or 1.0; therefore, adding $0.\bar{1}$ to itself nine times should also yield 1.0. Hence, $0.\bar{1} + 0.\bar{1} + 0.\bar{1} + 0.\bar{1} + 0.\bar{1} + 0.\bar{1} + 0.\bar{1} + 0.\bar{1} + 0.\bar{1} = 0.\bar{9} = 1.0$.[9] And so the infinitely repeating decimal proves finite after all. Or, from another perspective, one might say that the infinite can be made to exist in and through the finite.

To help us pursue this latter suggestion, let us compare the way some irrational numbers are represented. For the purposes of this paper, I will define irrationals as those numbers that cannot be expressed as belonging to $\mathbf{Q} = \{x \mid x = a/b, b \neq 0\}$. I understand that one is at least partly on her way to representing irrational numbers when she writes non-repeating, non-terminating decimals.[10] That certain of these numbers prove so important to everyday usage is indicative that at least some non-terminating decimal cases might have theoretical consequences. Two ancient examples might be adduced: the values π and $\sqrt{2}$.[11]

Ancient geometers, through their work with proportions, believed there were common ratios that could explain why geometric shapes of different sizes could be what we might call "similar," a relation where

---

8. Compare Vilenkin, *Infinity*, 72–74.

9. An article on repetends that includes this argument along with its algebraic proof can be found online. See "How to Make a Repetend."

10. One may prefer "any number that cannot be the solution to a first order equation whose coefficients are integers" or a similar algebraic formulation. I prefer the traditional definition that includes the transcendental numbers π and e, etc.

11. The two values are of historical import since the former is a transcendental and the latter is not. Still, both values are ubiquitous. π, especially, has peculiar properties. According to Zerbrowski, ten percent of its non-repeating, non-terminating decimals are ones, ten percent twos, and so on. Truly fascinating! See Zebrowski, *History*, 11.

the measures of corresponding angles between polygons could remain equal while the proportions between the measures of corresponding sides would adhere to a common ratio.[12] The two irrational examples of π and √2 are ratios that involve two very common geometric shapes. π is the ratio of the circumference of a circle to its diameter. All circles have this ratio; all circles are similar. √2 is the length of the diagonal of a square with a side length one. It can be generalized as the ratio of the diagonal of any square to any of its sides. Since all squares are similar, what we might say about √2 would also apply to what we might say about squares generally. I posit the analogous scenario for circles: whatever might be said about π would also apply to what we might say about circles generally.

Aristotle averred that his arguments against an actual infinite did "not rob the mathematicians of their science." He observed, for example: "In point of fact [the mathematicians] do not need the infinite and do not use it. They postulate only that the finite straight line may be produced as far as they wish."[13] He can say this because ancient geometers, according to Aristotle, would always restrict their work to "real magnitudes."[14] In other words, mathematicians live and work in the same world that everyone else does and since actual infinites do not exist, geometers are only really dealing with finite magnitudes.

Since Aristotle's time, there have been a number of important developments in mathematics. Geometry, in particular, has been wholly restructured so that practitioners no longer start with a hypothetically infinite space within which a line can be extended "as far as they wish." Rather, one starts with a single point. Space is created as points are added—as *many* as they wish—and the type of space created corresponds to the type of geometry employed. In any event, geometry has long since been arithmetically conceived, and the existence of a line requires some kind of continuum, and the existence of a circle or a square requires the existence of the ratios of π and √2. If actual infinites are not allowed, then it would appear that the geometric figures that utilize these notions for their construction would also be disallowed.

---

12. Fowler has challenged our common understanding of early Greek mathematics. For our purposes, it does not matter whether early Greek geometers thought of ratios in this way or not. See Fowler, *Mathematics*.

13. Aristotle, *Physics*, 3.7.

14. Whether he was thinking in terms of numbers or units, the result is the same. See Fowler, *Mathematics*.

Ideas at the Intersection of Mathmatics, Philosophy, and Theology

Are we presuming here the existence of numbers and (perhaps worse) that of segments, circles and squares? The concern with the latter is that actual measurements that humans draw are sloppy and could never be carried out with the kind of precision necessary for our actual infinites to obtain. If lines, circles, squares, and π and √2 do not exist in the real world, all of this is moot. Compare Augustine's response in the *City of God* to those who had trouble believing that God created the world from outside of time, where he compares those who postulate an infinite past with those who postulate an infinite space: "Of course, they may admit that it is silly to imagine infinite space since there is no such thing as space beyond the cosmos. In that case, let this be the answer: It is silly for them to excogitate a past time during which God was unoccupied, for the simple reason that there was no such thing as time before the universe was made."[15] However, in terms of the present discussion, can the existence of π and √2 be denied on the basis that actual infinites do not exist? Or, conversely, can actual infinites be supposed to exist on the basis of actual infinites such as π and √2? Platonism is not the only way out of this since an Aristotelian predilection for particulars (in this case particular infinites) remains a live option for understanding what it might mean for an actual infinite to exist.

It is interesting to observe that both those who uphold the existence of the actual infinite and those who deny its existence charge the other side with confusing potential and actual infinites.[16] Perhaps the reason for this is that both sides have different senses of "exist" in mind and are applying them to the same actual infinites. Craig argues that an actual infinite cannot exist. But what does "exist" mean here? Is an actual infinite a mathematical entity?[17] If so, we should inquire after whether mathematical entities can exist. If they happen to exist, *in what way* do we say that they exist? Do they exist in the same way that my hard copy of Euclid's

---

15. Augustine, *City of God*, (trans. G. G. Walsh), 211.
16. See, for example, Oderberg, "Traversal," 319–20.
17. What is a mathematical entity anyway? Most people think of math as being primarily concerned with *numbers*—and even this comes in two varieties. Those less familiar with (pure) mathematics understand numbers as quantities, and those more familiar with it see numbers as concepts. Oftentimes, I cannot help but think that mathematics is not concerned with numbers at all. (After all, how many classes are there during which the only numbers used are those that are put on the board to signify the date?) Perhaps Russell was on to something when he suggested that mathematics is primarily concerned with *order*, or Shapiro in his emphasis on *structure*.

Elements exists? Or in the way that my digital copy exists? Do they exist in the way propositions exist or perhaps in the way fictions do?

Do they exist in the same way that an abstract, "perfect" circle (which can never be constructed) exists? Or perhaps in more than one of these ways? Or in some other way altogether? A number of ontological questions come to mind. Each of these ways of "existing" (or non-existing) would be compared to the way that time is said to "exist." The reason Craig and Smith discuss this topic at all is to see how it might bear on the (hypothetical) existence of an infinite time past. Recall Craig's A1 and A3:

A1. An actual infinite cannot exist.

A3. An *infinite* temporal regress cannot exist.

Craig's suggestion is that the infinite in A1 "exists" in the same way as that of the infinite in A3. Is this necessarily so? Might there be another way?

Craig's absurdities explore whether a temporal regress can exist in precisely the same manner that a library or hotel exists and, moreover, whether all actual infinites would exist in the same way. Is Craig conflating several senses of exist? For example, does the absurdity that arises when a book is added to an infinite library suggest, at most, that there are no infinite libraries? Do the problems that arise if there is an infinite amount of gold in the universe suggest, at most, that there is not an infinite amount of gold in the universe?[18] Do Craig's examples metaphysically preclude the actual infinite out of court? Craig does not appear to be arguing from induction but rather making an argument based on the parity of reasoning. Still, one might hold that Craig's absurdities *are* objectionable and still conclude that they merely show how *particular*, actual infinites do not exist in particular ways. If the postulation of an infinite amount of gold leads to absurdities, then there is not an infinite amount of gold in the universe. If the postulation of a library with infinite books leads to absurdity, then there is no library with infinite books. The same goes for the gentleman who attempts his autobiography.[19] If a negative verdict is arrived at, that would only settle the question of whether that actual infinite existed in that particular way.

Yet Craig seeks to accomplish more through his examples. The absurdities he discusses are meant to suggest that there is no end to the

18. See Thomson, "Infinity," 4.184–185.
19. Compare Oderberg, "Traversal."

inane scenarios one can imagine. This suggests the conclusion that actual infinites cannot be said to exist anywhere in the physical universe. But one does not necessarily have to draw this conclusion, do they? One might take a second look at A1 and suggest it be emended to read:

> A1´. An actual infinite cannot exist in the physical world in the same way that a library or hotel, etc. exists in the physical world.

Then A2 might be appended to the effect that it should read:

> A2´. Time exists in the world in the same way that a library or hotel, etc. exists in the physical world.

Perhaps then Craig would be in a position to claim:

> A3´. An infinite temporal regress cannot exist.

This seems more reasonable and appears to be more in line with what Craig actually argues since he allows for other types of actual infinites to exist in other ways.

It bears mentioning that not all philosophers who believe that God created the world think that there could not be an infinite past. While making his case, Craig surveys the historical landscape and picks and chooses elements from different writers that comport well with his thesis. For example, he commends the minority intuitionist school for their insight into the infinite but he denies the intuitionist tenets that accompany this insight. Craig also relies heavily on Aristotle's distinction between an actual infinite and a potential infinite, but he denies Aristotle's conclusion that the universe is eternal. Craig also fails to mention that Thomas Aquinas—who did more than anyone in the history of Christian thought to reconcile Aristotelianism with Christianity—admitted that reason, left to itself, is simply not able to decide between Aristotle's position and the Church's on this question of an infinite past.[20] Among modern authors, Keith Ward suggests that Christians are not forced to decide between an eternal universe and a finite universe. Richard Swinburne concedes similar ground: the universe might not have had a beginning.[21] Whether

---

20. See, for example, Aquinas, *Summa Contra Gentiles*, 2.38, among other places.
21. Ward, *God*, 15–33; Swinburne, *Providence*, ix.

Observations regarding the Kalam argument

the universe had a beginning or not seems debatable, a point not settled amongst believers.

What about the absurdities? One might counter with something like Augustine's response above: What about π and √2? In my view, π and √2 exist in the physical world. Comprising actual infinites as they do, they attend the instantiation of every circle and square.[22] The continuum, too, accompanies the instantiation of every line segment. The non-repeating decimals are "present" in *every* circle and square. The continuum is present in every line segment. If someone objects that there are no circles or squares, we can take solace in the fact that Platonism is not the only way out. Without appealing to "circles" and "squares" out there somewhere or in the mind, could one not hold that universals are present in the physical world, precisely in the case of every instantiation without its existing apart from them? By virtue of the representation of π and √2, *inter alia*, one might infer that the actual infinites involved in common ratios are part and parcel of the physical world.

Also relevant is the matter of transfinite arithmetic, which one could just as easily disavow without surrendering actual infinites.[23] It is interesting to note that at least some of the early Church Fathers might seem to have something like transfinite arithmetic in mind in their reflections of the Trinity. I have not come across the ancient puzzles surrounding the Trinity in the philosophical literature that treats this arm of the Kalam cosmological argument. But consider the following. How can Christians affirm that God the Father is not greater than God the Spirit? How can God the Father and God the Son together not be greater than God the Spirit? How can God the Father, God the Son and God the Spirit together not be greater than God the Spirit? (This paradox arises for each person of the godhead.) Do not Craig's paradoxes pop up here, too? Consider also the Incarnation. How did God the Son "exist" in the human Jesus? Did the Son (or any other person(s) of the Godhead) actually or potentially exist in Jesus? My own understanding of perichoresis is such that the Father, Son and Spirit must have all "existed" in the human being Jesus somehow since wherever the Son is the Father and Spirit are also. (Hopefully,

---

22. And what of sine and cosine and other periodic functions whose graphs depend on π? Special triangles involving √2, √3 also come to mind. *e* is another value one might consider.

23. Compare Oppy, "Inverse Operations."

I am not conflating the divine "persons" with the divine "substance.")[24] If the finite human being Jesus Christ is able to accommodate the actual infinite (God the Son) in the incarnation, must not physical reality somehow or in some way be able to instantiate actual infinity, paradoxes notwithstanding?

Craig's paradoxes involving transfinite arithmetic resemble the *sorites* puzzle. Compare the following:

1. α is an infinite number.

2. If one were to add or subtract k from α, the sum/difference would still be infinite.

3. $\alpha \pm k$ is an infinite number.

Can this line of thinking be carried out *ad infinitum* and lead to a *reductio ad absurdum*? Perhaps one of the reasons both Craig and Smith accuse the other of mistaking potential infinites for actual ones is that the concept "infinite" is vague to begin with. In terms of the *sorites* analogy, Craig and those who agree with him would be arguing essentially that there are no heaps. The other side would be arguing that there are heaps. But if the concept of "infinite" is vague then the distinction between potential and actual infinites becomes obscured.[25] Set theorists, among others, tend to consider the problem of the infinite solved, yet the idea of the infinite is still beset with enough conceptual vagueness that paradoxes (such as the ones Craig discusses) still arise.

If this is right, then Craig's (and others') argument to the effect of A1–A3 would really be better phrased as follows:

A1''. Actual infinites cannot be apprehended without paradox from within space-time.

A2''. Human beings exist in space-time.

A3''. Human beings cannot apprehend actual infinites without paradox.

---

24. Compare Augustine: "Just as the Trinity wrought that human form from the Virgin Mary; yet it is the person of the Son alone; for the invisible Trinity wrought the visible person of the Son alone" (*De Trin* 2.10—although he does concede that both the Father and the Son must have sent the Son).

25. Thomson proposes collapsing this distinction in Thomson, "Infinity."

Paradoxes may not be enough in this case to conclude that infinites are impossible.[26] Paradoxes may very well indicate that actual infinites are possible; it is just that humans cannot apprehend them adequately from their standpoint within space-time. In fact, when it comes to actual infinites, paradoxes might even be what one would expect. Paradoxes in this case might persuade that the actual infinites *are* real, even if human beings cannot adequately apprehend what it is they have encountered.[27]

In this chapter, I offered reflections on the debate in *TABC* regarding when an infinite amount of time can be said to exist. I tried to present Craig's argument syllogistically and raise problems with both the major premise and conclusion by considering whether the major premise might be true since there seem to be actual cases of the infinite in everyday, non-terminating decimals. I further suggested that some of these non-terminating decimals are instantiated in basic geometric figures. I went on to remark that Craig's conclusion that actual infinites do not exist may not *necessarily* follow from his premises. It may be the case that the existence of actual infinites should be conceptually or metaphysically ruled out because of the paradoxes that arise, but to *show* this may take a little more work.[28]

---

26. Am I only biding time? Have I devised an infinite-of-the-gaps argument? Perhaps, but sometimes, in spite of absurdities, certain ideas turn out to be more durable than they at first appeared. For the case of negative and complex numbers, see Jones, "Role."

27. Compare Moore, *Infinite*.

28. This paper was presented at the biannual meeting of the Association of Christians in Mathematical Sciences held at Messiah College, Grantham, Pennsylvania, May, 2007.

Bibliography

Abraham, William. *Canon and Criterion in Christian Theology: From the Fathers to Feminism*. New York: Oxford University Press, 1998.

Aquinas, Thomas. *Commentary to Posterior Anayltics*. The Logic Museum. http://www.logicmuseum.com/authors/aquinas/posterioranalytics/aquinasPA.htm (accessed April 10, 2012).

Azzouni, Jodi. "Thick Epistemic Access: Distinguishing the Mathematical from the Empirical." *Journal of Philosophy* 94 (1997): 472–484.

Bombardieri, Marcella. "Real-world Studies Proposed at Harvard." *Boston Globe* February 7, 2007. http://www.boston.com/news/local/articles/2007/02/08/real_world_studies_proposed_at_harvard/ (accessed April 10, 2012).

Berkeley, George. "George Berkeley's Criticisms of the Calculus." In *The History of Mathematics: A Reader*, edited by J. Fauvel and J. Gray, 556–558. New York: Palgrave Macmillan, 1987.

Bernet, Rudolf, Ido Kern, and Eduard Marbach. *An Introduction to Husserlian Phenomenology*. Evanston, IL: Northwestern University Press, 1993.

Blay, Michel. *Reasoning with the Infinite: From the Closed World to the Mathematical Universe*. Translated by M. B. DeBevoise. Chicago: University of Chicago Press, 1998.

Boiler, Paul F. *American Thought in Transition: The Impact of Evolutionary Naturalism, 1865–1900*. New York: University Press of America, 1981.

BonJour, Laurence, and Ernest Sosa. *Epistemic Justification: Internalism Vs. Externalism, Foundations Vs. Virtues*. Malden, MA: Blackwell Publishing, 2003.

Bovell, Carlos. *By Good and Necessary Consequence: A Preliminary Genealogy of Biblicist Foundationalism*. Eugene, OR: Wipf and Stock, 2009.

Boyer, Carl. *The History of the Calculus and Its Conceptual Development*. New York: Dover Publications, 1949.

Bozeman, Theodore Dwight. *Protestants in an Age of Science: The Baconian Ideal and Antebellum American Religious Thought*. Chapel Hill: University of North Carolina, 1977.

Brisson, Luc, and F. W. Meyerstein. *Inventing the Universe: Plato's "Timaeus," the Big Bang, and the Problem of Scientific Knowledge*. Albany, NY: State University of New York Press, 1995.

Brooke, John Hedley. *Science and Religion: Some Historical Perspectives*. New York: Cambridge University Press, 1991.

Brown, Theodore. *Making Truth: Metaphor in Science*. Champaign, IL: University of Illinois Press, 2003.

Burns, Jim. "Aren't Miracles Magic?" *Campus Life* 69.9 (June/July 2004): 22.

Butterworth, Brian. *What Counts: How Every Brain is Hard-wired for Math*. New York: Free Press, 1999.

Bibliography

Byers, William. *How Mathematicians Think: Using Ambiguity, Contradiction, and Paradox to Create Mathematics*. Princeton, NJ: Princeton University Press, 2007.

Cairns, Dorion. *Conversations with Husserl and Fink*. New York: Springer, 1976.

Cantor, Georg. "Contributions to the Founding of the Theory of Transfinite Numbers." In *God Created the Integers: the Mathematical Breakthroughs That Changed History*, edited by S. Hawking, 971–1040. Philadelphia: Running Press, 2007.

Cartwright, Richard. *Philosophical Essays*. Cambridge, MA: MIT Press, 1987.

Centrone, Stefania. *Logic and Philosophy of Mathematics in the Early Husserl*. Dordrecht: Springer, 2010.

Chaitin, Gregory. *Meta Math! The Quest for Omega*. New York: Vintage Books, 2005.

Chandler, Albert. "Professor Husserl's Program of Philosophic Reform." *Philosophical Review* 26 (1917): 634–648.

Chemero, Anthony. *Radical Embodied Cognitive Science*. Cambridge, MA: MIT Press, 2009.

Clarke, Arthur. "Credo." In *Science and Religion: Are They Compatible?*, edited by Paul Kurtz, 181–187. Amherst, NY: Prometheus, 2003.

Clayton, Philip. *God and Contemporary Science*. Grand Rapids: Eerdmans, 1997.

———. "Natural Law and Divine Action: The Search for an Expanded Theory of Causation." *Zygon* 39 (2004): 615–636.

Craig, William Lane, and Quentin Smith. *Theism, Atheism and Big Bang Cosmology*. New York: Oxford University Press, 1993.

Dahlstrom, Daniel. *Heidegger's Concept of Truth*. New York: Cambridge University Press, 2001.

Dauben, Joseph. "C. S. Peirce's Philosophy of Infinite Sets." *Mathematics Magazine* 50.3 (1977): 123–135.

———. *Georg Cantor: His Mathematics and Philosophy of the Infinite*. Princeton: Princeton University Press, 1979.

Davis, Philip. "Number." In *Mathematics in the Modern World: Readings from Scientific American*, edited by M. Kline, 89-97. San Francisco: W. H. Freeman and Company, 1968.

Davis, Stephen T. *Logic and the Nature of God*. Grand Rapids: Eerdmans, 1983.

Dedekind, Richard. "Dedekind on Irrational Numbers and the Theorems of the Calculus." In *The History of Mathematics: A Reader*, edited by J. Fauvel and J. Gray, 573–577. New York: Palgrave Macmillan, 1987.

Dehaene, Stanislas. *The Number Sense: How the Mind Creates Mathematics*. New York: Oxford University Press, 1997.

Descartes, Rene. *Discourse on Method*. Johnstonia. http://records.viu.ca/~johnstoi/Descartes/descartes1.htm (accessed April 10, 2012).

———. *Meditations and Other Metaphysical Writings*. Translated by D. M. Clarke. New York: Penguin, 1998.

Devlin, Keith. *The Math Gene: How Mathematical Thinking Evolved and Why Numbers Are Like Gossip*. New York: Basic Books, 2000.

Dewey, John. *The Influence of Darwin on Philosophy and Other Essays*. Amherst, NY: Prometheus, 1997.

Dieks, Dennis. "The Flexibility of Mathematics." In *The Role of Mathematics in Physical Science: Interdisciplinary and Philosophical Aspects*, edited by G. Boniolo, P. Budinich, and M. Trobok, 115–129. Dordrecht: Springer, 2005.

Bibliography

Dreyfus, Hubert. *Being-in-the-World: A Commentary on Heidegger's "Being and Time," Division I*. Cambridge, MA: MIT Press, 1991.
Dummett, Michael. *The Nature and Future of Philosophy*. New York: Columbia University Press, 2010.
———. "What is Mathematics?" In *Mathematics and Mind*, edited by A. George, 1–26. New York: Oxford University Press, 1994.
Eccles, Peter. *An Introduction to Mathematical Reasoning: Numbers, Sets and Functions*. New York: Cambridge University Press, 1997.
Edwards, Harold. "Kronecker's Place in History." In *History and Philosophy of Modern Mathematics*, edited by W. Aspray and P. Kitcher, 139–144.Minneapolis: University of Minnesota Press, 1988.
Elden, Stuart. "The Place of Geometry: Heidegger's Mathematical Excursus on Aristotle." *Heythrop Journal* 42 (2010): 311–328.
Faye, Emmanuel. *Heidegger: The Introduction of Nazism into Philosophy*. Translated by Michael B. Smith. New Haven, CT: Yale University Press, 2009.
Feinberg, John. *No One Like Him*. Wheaton, IL: Crossway, 2001.
Field, Hartry. "Is Mathematical Knowledge Just Logical Knowledge?" *The Philosophical Review* 93 (1984): 509–552.
Filosofiska Institutionen. "Skepticism in Medieval and Renaissance Thought." Uppsala Universitet. http://info.uu.se/konferens.nsf/id/2005-05-06.skepticism.in.html (accessed April 10, 2012).
Finocchiaro, Maurice. "Galileo and the Philosophy of Science." *PSA: Proceedings of the Biennial Meeting of the Philosophy of Science Association* 1 (1976): 130–139.
———. "Philosophizing about Galileo." *British Journal for the Philosophy of Science* 26 (1975): 255–64.
———. "Review of *'Galileo's Pendulum'* by Dušan I. Bjelić." *Isis* 95 (2004): 754–755.
Fowler, D. H. *The Mathematics of Plato's Academy: A New Reconstruction*. 2nd ed. New York: Oxford, 1999.
Franzén, Torkel. *Gödel's Theorem: An Incomplete Guide to Its Use and Abuse*. Wellesley, MA: A K Peters, 2005.
Frege, Gottleb. *The Foundations of Arithmetic*. 2nd ed. Translated by J. L. Austin. Malden: Blackwell, 1980.
Galilei, Galileo. *Dialogues Concerning Two New Sciences*. Philadelphia: Running Press, 2007.
Gallagher, Shaun, and Dan Zahavi. *The Phenomenological Mind: An Introduction to Philosophy of Mind and Cognitive Science*. New York: Routledge, 2008.
García Prado, Ovidio. "La fundamentación de la matemática y la génesis de la métodica fenomenológico-reductiva." *Anales del Seminario de Historia de la Filosofía* 6 (1986–1989): 47–78.
Geach, Peter. *Logic Matters*. Berkeley, CA: University of California Press, 1972.
Glazebrook, Trish. *Heidegger's Philosophy of Science*. New York: Fordham University Press, 2000.
Gold, Bonnie. "Review of *'Where Mathematics Comes From'* by Lakoff and Nuñez." The MAA Mathematical Sciences Digital Library. http://mathdl.maa.org/mathDL/19/?pa=reviews&sa=viewBook&bookId=68976l (accessed April 10, 2012).
Gold, Bonnie and Roger Simons, *Proof and Other Dilemmas: Mathematics and Philosophy*. Washington, D.C.: Mathematical Association of America, 2008.

Bibliography

Goldsworthy, Graeme. "Relationship of the Old Testament and New Testament." In *New Dictionary of Biblical Theology: Exploring the Unity and Diversity of Scripture*, edited by T. Desmond Alexander, et al., 82–83. Downers Grove, IL: InterVarsity, 2000.

Gouvêa, Fernando. "Review of '*What Is Mathematics, Really?*' by Reuben Hersh." The MAA Mathematical Sciences Digital Library. http://www.maa.org/reviews/whatis.html (accessed April 10, 2012).

Gray, Jeremy. *Plato's Ghost: The Modernist Transformation of Mathematics*. Princeton, NJ: Princeton University Press, 2008.

Grene, Marjorie. *Philosophy in and out of Europe*. Lanham, MD: University Press of America, 1987.

Griffin, David Ray. *Religion and Scientific Naturalism: Overcoming the Conflicts*. Albany, NY: State University of New York, 2000.

Grozdev, Sava, Ivan Derzhanski, and Evgenia Sendova. "For Those Who Think Mathematics Dreary." *Dnevnik* 1.238, 27 December 2001. http://www.math.bas.bg/ml/iad/dreamt/dmathen.html.

Gyekye, Kwame. "Al-Farabi on the Logic of the Arguments of the Muslim Philosophical Theologians." *Journal of the History of Philosophy* 27 (1989): 135–143.

Hadot, Pierre. *Philosophy as a Way of Life*. Edited by A. I. Davidson. Translated by M. Chase. Malden, MA: Blackwell, 1995.

Hahn, Hans. "Geometry and Intuition." In *Mathematics in the Modern World: Readings from Scientific American*, edited by M. Kline, 184–189. San Francisco: W. H. Freeman and Company, 1968.

Happel, Stephen. "Divine Providence and Instrumentality: Metaphors for Time in Self-Organizing Systems and Divine Action." In *Chaos and Complexity: Scientific Perspectives on Divine Action*. 2nd ed., edited by R. J. Russell, N. Murphy, and A. R. Peacocke, 177–203. Berkeley, CA: The Center for Theology and the Natural Sciences, 2000.

Harries, Karsten. *Infinity and Perspective*. Cambridge, MA: The MIT Press, 2001.

Hart, J. G. "A Précis of an Husserlian Philosophical Theology." In *Essays in Phenomenological Theology*, edited by S. W. Laycock and J. G. Hart. Albany, NY: State University of New York Press, 1986.

Hartimo, Mirja. "Towards Completeness: Husserl on Theories of Manifolds 1890-1901." *Synthese* 156 (2007): 281–310.

Hartshorne, Charles. *Creative Synthesis and Philosophic Method*. LaSalle, IL: Open Court Publishing, 1970.

Heidegger, Martin. *Being and Time*. Translated by J. Stambaugh. Albany, NY: State University of New York Press, 1996.

———. *Introduction to Metaphysics*. Translated by Ralph Manheim. New York: Doubleday, 1961.

———. "What is Metaphysics?" In *Basic Writings: From "Being and Time" (1927) to "The Task of Thinking" (1964)*, edited by D. F. Krell, 91–112. New York: Harper and Row, 1977.

Hendricks, Vincent, and Hannes Leitgeb. *Philosophy of Math: 5 Questions*. Birkerød, Denmark: Automatic Press, 2008.

Hersh, Rueben. "Review of '*How Mathematicians Think*' by William Byers." American Mathematical Society. http://www.ams.org/notices/200711/tx071101496p.pdf (accessed April 10, 2012).

Bibliography

Herron, Timothy. "C. S. Peirce's Theories of Infinitesimals." *Transactions of the Charles S. Peirce Society* 33 (1997): 590–645.

Hetherington, Stephen. "Fallibilism." The Internet Encyclopedia of Philosophy. http://www.iep.utm.edu/g/gettier.htm#H3 (accessed April 10, 2012).

———. *Good Knowledge, Bad Knowledge: On Two Dogmas of Epistemology*. New York: Oxford University Press, 2002.

———. "Knowledge's Boundary Problem." *Synthese* 150 (2006): 41–56.

Hibbs, Thomas. "Kretzmann's Theism vs Aquinas's Theism: Interpreting the *Summa Contra Gentiles*" *The Thomist* 62 (1998): 603–622.

Hilbert, David. "Extract from Hilbert's Göttingen Lectures." In *From Kant to Hilbert: A Sourcebook in the Foundations of Mathematics*, edited by W. Ewald, 2.943–946. New York: Oxford University Press, 1996.

———. "On the Infinite." In *Philosophy of Mathematics*, edited by Paul Benacerraf and Hilary Putnam, 183–201. New York: Cambridge University Press, 1983.

Howell, Russell, and W. James Bradley. *Mathematics in a Postmodern Age: A Christian Perspective*. Grand Rapids: Eerdmans, 2001.

Hurtado, Larry. *At the Origins of Christian Worship: The Context and Character of Earliest Christian Devotion*. Grand Rapids: Eerdmans, 1999.

Husserl, Edmund. *Husserl: Shorter Works*. Edited by P. McCormick and F. Elliston. Notre Dame, IN: Notre Dame University Press, 1981.

———. *Logical Investigations, Volume 1*. Translated by J. N. Findlay. New York: Routledge, 1970.

———. *The Crisis of European Science and Transcendental Phenomenology: An Introduction to Phenomenological Philosophy*. Translated by D. Carr. Evanston, IL: Northwestern University Press, 1970.

Hyde, Dominic. "Why Higher Order Vagueness is a Pseudo-Problem." *Mind* 103 (1994): 35–41.

Insall, Matt, and Eric Weisstein. "Nonstandard Analysis." Wolfram Research. http://mathworld.wolfram.com/NonstandardAnalysis.html (accessed April 10, 2012).

Jagerschmid, Adelgundis. "Conversations with Husserl, 1931–1938." *The New Yearbook for Phenomenology and Phenomenological Philosophy* I (2001): 331–350.

Jones, P. S. "The Role in the History of Mathematics of Algorithms and Analogies." In *Learn from the Masters* , edited by F. Swetz, J. Fauvel, et al., 13–23. Washington, D.C.: Mathematical Association of America, 1995.

Joseph, G. C. *The Crest of the Peacock: Non-European Roots of Mathematics*. 2nd ed. Princeton, NJ: Princeton University Press, 2000.

Kelly, J. N. D. *Early Christian Doctrines*. Revised edition. New York: HarperCollins, 1978.

Kline, Morris. *Mathematics: The Loss of Certainty*. New York: Oxford University Press, 1980.

———. *Mathematics for the Nonmathematician*. Mineola, NY: Dover Publications, 1985.

Kockelmans, Joseph. "The Mathematization of Nature in Husserl's Last Publication, *Krisis*." In *Phenomenology and the Natural Sciences: Essays and Translations*, edited by J. Kockelmans and T. Kisiel, 45–67. Evanston, IL: Northwestern University Press, 1970.

Korey, Jane. "Dartmouth College Mathematics across the Curriculum Evaluation Summary: Mathematics and Humanities Courses." Department of Mathematics at Dartmouth. http://www.math.dartmouth.edu/~matc/Evaluation/humeval.pdf (accessed April 10, 2012).

Bibliography

Lakoff, George, and Rafael Nuñez. "Reader Review." The MAA Mathematical Sciences Digital Library. http://mathdl.maa.org/mathDL/19/?pa=reviews&sa=viewReview&bookId =68976&reviewId=82 (accessed April 10, 2012).

———. *Where Mathematics Comes From: How the Embodied Mind Brings Mathematics into Being*. New York: Basic Books, 2000.

Lamont, Michèle. *How Professors Think: Inside the Curious World of Academic Judgment*. Cambridge, MA: Harvard University Press, 2009.

Lange, John. *Cognitivity Paradox: An Inquiry Concerning the Claims of Philosophy*. Princeton, NJ: Princeton University Press, 1970.

Lawhead, William. *The Philosophical Journey: An Interactive Approach*. 4th ed. New York: McGraw-Hill, 2008.

Lee, Jung Young. *The Trinity in Asian Perspective*. Nashville: Abingdon, 1996.

Leibniz, Gottfried. *Philosophical Essays*. Indianapolis, IN: Hackett Publishing Company, 1989.

Levering, Matthew. *Scripture and Metaphysics: Aquinas and the Renewal of Trinitarian Theology*. Malden, MA: Blackwell, 2004.

Lewis, Clarence Irving. *Mind and the World Order: Outline of a Theory of Knowledge*. New York: Dover Publications, 1956.

Lockhart, Paul. *A Mathematician's Lament*. New York: Bellevue Literary Press, 2009.

Lonergan, Bernard. *Method in Theology*. Toronto: University of Toronto Press, 1990.

———. *Phenomenology and Logic*. Toronto: University of Toronto Press, 2001.

Lubański, Mieczyslaw. "Galileo's View on Infinity." In *The Galileo Affair: A meeting of faith and science, Proceedings of the Cracow Conference, May 24–27, 1984*, edited by G. Coyne, 125–136. Citta del Vaticano: Specola Vaticana, 1985.

Lucas, J. R. *Conceptual Roots of Mathematics*. New York: Routledge, 2001.

Mac Lane, Saunders. *Mathematics: Form and Function*. New York: Springer-Verlag, 1986.

Machamer, Peter. "Galileo Galilei." In *The Stanford Encyclopedia of Philosophy*, edited by E. Zalta. http://plato.stanford.edu/archives/spr2010/entries/galileo/.

Maor, Eli. *To Infinity and Beyond: A Cultural History of the Infinite*. Princeton, NJ: Princeton University Press, 1987.

Marion, Jean-Luc. *On Descartes' Metaphysical Prism: The Constitution and the Limits of Onto-Theo-Logy in Cartesian Thought*. Translated by J. L. Kosky. Chicago: The University of Chicago Press, 1999.

Martinez, Alberto. *Negative Math: How Mathematical Rules Can Be Positively Bent*. Princeton, NJ: Princeton University Press, 2006.

Marx, Werner. *Heidegger and the Tradition*. Translated by T. Kisiel and M. Greene. Evanston, IL: Northwestern University Press, 1971.

Merleau-Ponty, Maurice. *Husserl at the Limits of Phenomenology Including Texts by Edmund Husserl*. Edited by L. Lawlor. Evanston, IL: Northwestern University Press, 2002.

de Montaigne, Michel. *The Complete Works of Montaigne*. Translated by D. M. Frame. Stanford, CA: Stanford University Press, 1958.

Moore, A. W. *The Infinite*. 2nd ed. New York: Routledge, 2001.

Moran, Dermot. "Heidegger's Transcendental Phenomenology in the Light of Husserl's Project of First Philosophy." In *Transcendental Heidegger*, edited by Steven Crowell and Jeff Malpas, 135–150. Stanford, CA: Stanford University Press, 2007.

Moreland, J. P. "Complementarity, Agency Theory, and God of the Gaps." *Perspectives on Science and Christian Faith* 49 (1997): 2–14.

———. "Theistic Science and Methodological Naturalism." In *Creation Hypothesis: Scientific Evidence for an Intelligent Designer*, edited by J. P. Moreland, 41–66. Downers Grove, IL: InterVarsity, 1994.

Moser, Paul. *Philosophy after Objectivity: Making Sense in Perspective*. New York: Oxford University Press, 1993.

Moyn, Samuel. *Origins of the Other: Emmanuel Levinas between Revelation and Ethics*. Ithaca, NY: Cornell University Press, 2005.

Muller, Richard A. "Inspired by God—Pure in All Ages: The Doctrine of Scripture in the Westminster Confession." In *Scripture and Worship: Biblical Interpretation and the Directory for Worship* by Richard A. Muller and Rowland Ward, 31–58. Phillipsburg, NJ: Presbyterian and Reformed Publishing, 2007.

Mura, Roberta. "Images of Mathematics Held by University Teachers of Mathematical Sciences." *Educational Studies in Mathematics* 25 (1993): 375–85.

Mycielski, Jan. "A System of Axioms of Set Theory for the Rationalists." *Notices of the AMS* 53.2 (2006): 206–213.

Natorp, Paul. "On the Question of Logical Method in Relation to Edmund Husserl's *Prolegomena to Pure Logic*." In *Edmund Husserl: Critical Assessments of Leading Philosophers*, edited by R. Bernet, D. Welton, and G. Zavota, 32–46. New York: Routledge, 2005.

Newton, Isaac. *Principia*. Philadelphia: Running Press Book Publishers, 2002.

Northrop, Filmer. "Einstein's Conception of Science." In *Albert Einstein: Philosopher-Scientist*, edited by P. A. Schilpp, 385–408. New York: M. J. F. Books, 1979.

O'Carroll, Michael. *Trinitas: A Theological Encyclopedia of the Holy Trinity*. Wilmington, DE: Michael Glazier, Inc., 1987.

O'Connor, J. J., and E. F. Robertson. "Leopold Kronecker." The School of Mathematics and Statistics at the University of St. Andrews. http://www-history.mcs.st-and.ac.uk/Biographies/Kronecker.html (accessed April 10, 2012).

Ockham, William. *Quodlibetal Questions: Quodlibets 1-7*. Translated by A. J. Freddoso and F. E. Kelley. New Haven, CT: Yale University Press, 1991.

Oderberg, D. S. "Traversal of the Infinite, the 'Big Bang,' and the KALAM Cosmological Argument." *Philosophia Christi* 4 (2002): 303–334.

Oppy, Graham. "Inverse Operations with Transfinite Numbers and the Kalam Cosmological Argument." *International Philosophical Quarterly* 35 (1999): 199–221.

Ortiz Hill, Claire, and G. E. Rosado Haddock. *Husserl or Frege? Meaning, Objectivity, and Mathematics*. Chicago: Open Court, 2000.

Ostebee, A., and P. Zorn. *Calculus from Graphical, Numerical, and Symbolic Points of View*. 2nd ed. New York: Houghton Mifflin Company, 2002.

Palevitz, Barry. "Science Versus Religion: A Conversation with My Students." In *Science and Religion: Are They Compatible?*, edited by Paul Kurtz, 171–179. Amherst, NY: Prometheus, 2003.

Parker, Matthew. "Philosophical Method and Galileo's Paradox of Infinity." In *New Perspectives on Mathematical Practices: Essays in Philosophy and History of Mathematics: Brussels, Belgium, 26-28 March 2007*, edited by B. van Kerkhove, 76–113. Hackensack, NJ: World Scientific Publishing, 2009.

Pascal, Blaise. *Pascal Selections*. Edited by R. Popkin. New York: Macmillian, 1989.

Pincock, Christopher. "Carnap's Logical Structure of the World." *Philosophy Compass* 4 (2009): 951–961.

Bibliography

Plantinga, Alvin. "Methodological Naturalism?" *Perspectives on Science and Christian Faith* 49 (1997): 143–154.

Polya, George. *How to Solve It*. Princeton, NJ: Princeton University Press, 1957.

Prestige, G. L. *God in Patristic Thought*. London: SPCK, 1959.

Quine, Willard V. O. *Ways of Paradox and Other Essays*. Cambridge, MA: Harvard University Press, 1976.

Raatikainen, Panu. "On the Philosophical Relevance of Gödel's Incompleteness Theorems." *Revue Internationale de Philosophie* 59 (2005): 513–534.

Redner, Harry. *The Ends of Philosophy: An Essay in the Sociology of Philosophy*. New York: Routledge, 1986.

Rescher, Nicholas. *Philosophical Dialectics*. Albany, NY: State University of New York Press, 2006.

Reynolds, John Mark. "God of the Gaps." In *Mere Creation: Science, Faith and Intelligent Design*, edited by William Dembski, 313–331. Downers Grove, IL: InterVarsity, 1998.

Rota, Gian-Carlo. "Ten Remarks on Husserl and Phenomenology." In *Phenomenology on Kant, German Idealism, Hermeneutics and Logic*, edited by O. Wiegand, R. Dostal, L. Embree, J. Kockelmans, and J. N. Mohaty, 89–97. Dordrecht, Netherlands: Kluwer Academic Publishers, 2000.

Rucker, Rudy. *The Lifebox, the Seashell, and the Soul: What Gnarly Computation Taught Me about Ultimate Reality, the Meaning of Life and how to Be Happy*. New York: Thunder's Mouth Press, 2006.

Ruelle, David. *Chance and Chaos*. Princeton, NJ: Princeton University Press, 1991.

Russell, Bertrand. *The Basic Writings of Bertrand Russell*. Edited by R. Egner and L. Denonn. New York: Simon and Schuster, 1961.

——. *The Principles of Mathematics*. New York: W. W. Norton, 1996.

Sagal, P. T. "Peirce on Infinitesimals." *Transactions of the Charles S. Peirce Society* 14 (1978): 132–135.

Salmon, Nathan. *Metaphysics, Mathematics, and Meaning: Philosophical Papers*. New York: Oxford University Press, 2005.

Sawyer, W. W. "Algebra." In *Mathematics in the Modern World: Readings from Scientific American*, edited by Morris Kline, 102–110. San Francisco: W. H. Freeman and Co., 1968.

Sebestik, Jan. "Husserl Readers of Bolzano." In *Husserl's Logical Investigations Reconsidered*, edited by D. Fisette, 59–81. Dordrecht, Netherlands: Kluwer Academic Publishers, 2003.

Sfard, Anna. "The Many Faces of Mathematics: Do Mathematicians and Researchers in Mathematics Education Speak about the Same Thing?" In *Mathematics Education as a Research Domain: A Search for Identity*, edited by A. Sierpinska and J. Kilpatrick, 491–512. Norwell, MA: Kluwer Academic Publishers, 1997.

Small, Christopher. "Reflections on Godel's Ontological Argument." Department of Statistics and Actuarial Science at the University of Waterloo. http://www.stats.uwaterloo.ca/~cgsmall/Godel.final.revision.PDF (accessed April 10, 2012).

Smart, Harold. "The Alleged Predicament of Logic." *Journal of Philosophy* 41 (1944): 598–604.

Sorenson, Roy. *Pseudo-Problems: How Analytic Philosophy Gets Done*. New York: Routledge, 1993.

de Spinoza, Benedict. *Tractatus Theologico-Politicus*. Edited by J. Israel. New York: Cambridge University Press, 2007.

Bibliography

Spivak, Michael. *Calculus on Manifolds: A Modern Approach to Classical Theorems of Advanced Calculus*. New York: Perseus Press, 1965.
Squires, E. J. "Quantum Theory—a Window to the World beyond Physics." In *Philosophy, Mathematics and Modern Physics: A Dialogue*, edited by E. Rudolph and I. O. Stamatescu, 92–103. New York: Springer-Verlag, 1994.
Stead, Christopher. *Divine Substance*. New York: Oxford University Press, 1977.
Steiner, George. *Martin Heidegger*. Chicago: University of Chicago Press, 1989.
Stone, Abraham. "Heidegger and Carnap on the Overcoming of Metaphysics." In *Martin Heidegger*, edited by Stephen Muhall, 217–244. Burlington, VT: Ashgate, 2006.
Strandberg, Malcom. "Religion and Science: Convergence?" MWPS. http://web.mit.edu/mwpstr/www/religion/religion.htm (accessed April 10, 2012).
Stroud, Barry. *The Significance of Philosophical Skepticism*. New York: Oxford University Press, 1984.
Swinburne, Richard. *Providence and the Problem of Evil*. New York: Oxford University Press, 1998.
Taminiaux, Jacques. *The Metamorphoses of Phenomenological Reduction*. Milwaukee, WI: Marquette University Press, 2004.
Tasić, Vladimir. *Mathematics and the Roots of Postmodern Thought*. New York: Oxford University Press, 2001.
Thomas, R. S. D. "Extreme Science: Mathematics as the Science of Relations as Such." In *Proof and Other Dilemmas: Mathematics and Philosophy*, edited by Bonnie Gold and Roger Simons, 245–264. Washington, D.C.: Mathematical Association of America, 2008.
Thomson, J. "Infinity in Mathematics and Logic." In *Encyclopedia of Philosophy*, edited by Paul Edwards, 4.183–190. New York: MacMillan, 1967.
Thompson, Evan. *Mind in Life: Biology, Phenomenology, and the Sciences of Mind*. Cambridge, MA: Harvard University Press, 2007.
Thurston, William. "On Proof and Progress in Mathematics." *Bulletin of the American Mathematical Society* 30 (1994): 161–177.
Tieszen, Richard. *Phenomenology, Logic, and the Philosophy of Mathematics*. New York: Cambridge University Press, 2005.
Vaidya, Anand Jayprakash. "The Metaphysical Foundation of Logic." *Journal of Philosophical Logic* 35 (2006): 179–182.
van Inwagen, Peter. *God, Knowledge and Mystery: Essays in Philosophical Theology*. Ithaca, NY: Cornell University Press, 1995.
Vilenkin, N. Ya. *In Search of Infinity*. Translated by Abe Shenitzer. Boston: Birkhäuser, 1995.
Vogel, Kurt. "Ries, Adam." In *New Dictionary of Scientific Biography*, 11.456–458. Detroit: Charles Scribner's Sons, 2008.
Wagner, Steven. "Logicism." In *Proof and Knowledge in Mathematics*, edited by M. Detlefsen, 38–64. New York: Routledge, 1992.
Ward, Keith. *God, Chance and Necessity*. Rockport, MA: OneWorld, 1996.
White, Leslie. "The Locus of Mathematical Reality: An Anthropological Footnote." *Philosophy of Science* 14 (1947): 289–303.
Wilberg, Jonah. "Review of *Heidegger and Logic* by Greg Shirley." Notre Dame Philosophical Reviews. http://ndpr.nd.edu/news/24506-heidegger-and-logic-the-place-of-l-243-gos-in-being-and-time/ (accessed April 10, 2012).

Bibliography

Williams, Michael. "Epistemology and the Mirror of Nature." In *Rorty and His Critics*, edited by Robert Brandom, 191–212. Malden, MA: Blackwell Publishing, 2000.

———. *Unnatural Doubts: Epistemological Realism and the Basis of Skepticism*. Princeton, NJ: Princeton University Press, 1996.

Williamson, Timothy. *The Philosophy of Philosophy*. Malden, MA: Blackwell Publishing, 2007.

Wolfram, Stephen. "Kurt Gödel's 100th Birthday." The NKS Forum. http://forum.wolframscience.com/showthread.php?threadid=1063 (accessed April 10, 2012).

Young, Davis A. *The Biblical Flood: A Case Study of the Church's Response to Extrabiblical Evidence*. Grand Rapids: Eerdmans, 1995.

Zebrowski Jr., E. *A History of the Circle: Mathematical Reasoning and the Physical Universe*. New Brunswick, NJ: Rutgers University Press, 1999.